THEY DON'T NEED TO
UNDERSTAND

RARE BIRD

LOS ANGELES, CALIF.

THEY DON'T NEED TO
UNDERSTAND

STORIES OF HOPE, FEAR, LOVE, LIFE & NEVER GIVING IN

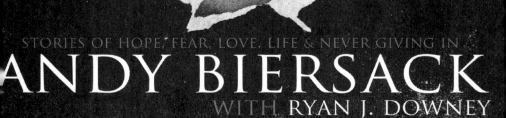

ANDY BIERSACK

WITH RYAN J. DOWNEY

THIS IS A GENUINE RARE BIRD BOOK

Rare Bird Books
453 South Spring Street, Suite 302
Los Angeles, CA 90013
rarebirdlit.com

Set in Dante
Printed in the United States

10 9 8 7 6 5 4 3 2 1

Interior design by Hailie Johnson

Publisher's Cataloging-in-Publication Data

Names: Biersack, Andy, author. | Downey, Ryan J., author.
Title: They Don't Need to Understand: Stories of Hope, Fear, Love,
Life, & Never Giving In / Andy Biersack with Ryan J. Downey.
Description: First Hardcover Edition | A Genuine Rare Bird Book |
New York, NY; Los Angeles, CA: Rare Bird Books, 2020.
Identifiers: ISBN 9781644281949
Subjects: LCSH Biersack, Andy. | Rock musicians—United States—
Biography. | Black Veil Brides (Musical group) | (Heavy metal (Music)
| Alternative metal (Music) | Rock music—2011–2020. |
BISAC BIOGRAPHY & AUTOBIOGRAPHY / Music
Classification: LCC ML420 .B538 2020 | DDC 782.42166/092—dc23

CONTENTS

INTRODUCTION

PLAYING HARD ROCK MUSIC in the past decade is a bit like going into an Apple store and trying to sell someone a flip phone. I know that I have been very fortunate to make rock records and tour the world in Black Veil Brides and with my solo vehicle, Andy Black.

The joke at the center of the Broadway musical *Rock of Ages* is the very *idea* of this music being "a thing." Hard rock, heavy metal, and punk rock are often considered antiquated, which honestly makes it sort of more rebellious than ever to try to become a rock singer.

Like many people who end up in the creative arts somewhere, I was a bit of a loner.

I built a version of myself from all of the things I feared when I was a child and presented it to the world as an adult. I'm a high school dropout and made most of my friends online.

I cofounded Black Veil Brides in my hometown and told everyone I would move to California when I turned eighteen. When the day arrived, nobody in the band came with me. It didn't matter. I moved from Cincinnati, Ohio, to Hollywood and lived in the back of my '98 Cadillac El Dorado because I wouldn't allow myself any other options. I *had* to make it.

There's a certain measure of being insufferable that's necessary for a story like mine. I'm an only child. I'd make my parents turn on the camcorder and read interview questions I'd prepared for myself. "Why, yes, Mom," I'd say as a precocious six-year-old. "I *am* the biggest rock star in the world right now, thank you so much for asking me about that."

I was determined to do something that, at least in the traditional sense, is essentially a non-"job," "work" that includes prancing around onstage in tight pants and eye makeup for a living. I wanted to tell stories with pageantry and art and to sing anthems for outcasts, idealists, and iconoclasts. It didn't matter that most people couldn't understand.

I put this book together with my good friend Ryan J. Downey, who has interviewed me via different mediums, in various settings, throughout my career. I'm sober now, which certainly helped as we rummaged through my memories, on multiple occasions, over lunch, dinner, or coffee, carving out afternoons and evenings between albums and tours.

It's sometimes hard to differentiate between what you remember happening as a very young kid and what you "remember" simply because an adult told you about it later.

I have a vivid picture of myself, as a baby, traveling with my mom when she was a make-up artist for Elizabeth Arden. (The skills my mom developed were of great use to me when I became interested in makeup as a teenager.) I don't "remember" that at all. But when those stories come up, I can paint a picture of exactly what that looked and felt like to experience. The images we portray for ourselves probably inform a lot more of our decisions than we realize, particularly among creative people who are already good at "painting pictures."

I knew that I wanted to create art and perform in a way that connected with people ever since I was a kid building tiny concerts in my bedroom with KISS action figures. The fact that I get to do precisely that as an adult makes me incredibly lucky. I'm not here to complain about how hard I had to work or proclaim what a martyr I am for living in my car and playing in basements and art galleries to "make it." I'd instead celebrate playing O2 Academy, Brixton, in London, surrounded by pyrotechnics, confetti, and five thousand fans.

My hope is there's something instructive in the work ethic it took to get here.

For the better part of the last ten years, I never sat down to think about whether or not I was enjoying myself. It was more about the constant push forward to prove to all the naysayers, real or perceived, that I was going to succeed and that I was going to do something great. As I've gained more perspective, it sometimes makes me laugh to remember how much of my adolescence and early adulthood was driven by revenge. I wanted vengeance against all of the people who didn't understand.

I'm not interested in telling a bunch of "rock guy" stories about how hard we partied. Even the stuff I engaged in that could be considered "rock 'n' roll debauchery" was less about who I was and more about falling into the role of someone I felt like I was *supposed* to be. I've come full circle. I'm back to my core, authentic self.

More than ever, I'm the same kid now as when I started, in so many ways. There were diversions from the path along the way, and yet here I am, back how I began.

I was barely eighteen years old the first time I went on tour. I was a high school dropout who moved to Hollywood to chase my rock 'n' roll dreams, but the truth is that at that age, I had no idea who I was as a person. I knew what I wanted to be, or at least the image I wanted to project. But I quickly found myself in a new world, a shifting reality, without the experience or wherewithal to navigate all of the challenges of life on the road.

I tried to replicate the behavior of my rock 'n' roll heroes I'd read about in an attempt to fit in with the older people around me. In 2020, as we arrived at the anniversary of our first album, *We Stitch These Wounds*, and the release of the reimagined version, *Re-Stitch These Wounds*, I found myself thinking back to those earliest days of Black Veil Brides. I would tell people I was nineteen in hopes they'd take me more seriously. I'd pretend I listened to "cool" and "important" bands because I was terrified of being treated like I wasn't cool.

I remember times I was rude or inconsiderate because I thought it made me seem more "interesting" or "badass." It takes time to find our way. It was a journey to become the person I'd started out dreaming I'd become. I never aspired to become a twenty-year-old jerk still shaking off the hangover from the night before, but as the influences around me grew stronger, that's where I quickly ended up. A character replaced my true self.

There are so many odds against an awkward kid from the Midwest becoming an internationally known performer. I never take it for granted that the fans are the reason I have that. I'm fortunate to have the love and adoration of even *one* person in a world where so many, from all walks of life, struggle to feel loved by anyone at all.

The ultimate goal was always to create something grand—a legacy. I've never been ashamed to say that I want success, even when the definition of "success" changes.

There's a stigma attached to doing "too much." I've been willing to do everything that's in front of me, whatever it takes, to achieve my goals. Complacency is the enemy.

This book isn't a "memoir," necessarily. (I'm too young for that.) I just want to explain as much as I can about how "this" happened in hopes that someone reading it will be able to draw inspiration from *my* story and feel encouraged to continue to build their own.

I'm also writing this to say thank you. Thank you for ten years of opportunities. Thank you for allowing me to evolve into a better person. Thanks for growing up with me, for singing with me, and for inspiring me. Because of you, I get the chance to do this all over again.

Now when I go on stage and perform these songs, both old and new, I'm not doing it from behind some "rock star" mask. I am doing it as an adult—a sober, married, comic book/sports nerd. And while that may not be the way all of my rock heroes were perceived, it turns out it is who I was meant to be. To me, that is my original rock 'n' roll dream come true.

1

GOLD & GODS

IT SHOULD HAVE BEEN a moment of triumph.

But the crowd booed us with visceral contempt. They *hated* Black Veil Brides.

The year before, in the same building, we were honored with a public seal of approval from a living legend, a man in black that had blazed a trail for every band like mine.

"I'm Alice Cooper. And I'm here to introduce the next performers that will grace the Golden Gods stage tonight." The pioneering shock rocker smiled widely at the fans filling the L.A. Live theater and everyone streaming the 2012 award show at home.

Our makeup made him as proud as our multiple nominations, he said.

"Rock 'n' roll right now is anemic," he pointed out. "Look at some of the bands out there. I keep telling them: you guys should just listen to Black Veil Brides."

The very next year, we were back at the Revolver Golden Gods Awards, a celebration of hard rock and heavy metal in downtown Los Angeles, listening to an introduction from *another* icon whose music we'd loved as kids. Sebastian Bach announced we had won "Song of the Year," making us the first band to earn a Golden God three times in a row. (Jake Pitts and Jinxx shared Best Guitarist in 2012; we were Best New Band in 2011.)

All of my rock 'n' roll dreams, my improbable but persistent plans, led to landmark accomplishments like that one. I was once a small boy in Cincinnati staging elaborate imaginary concerts in my bedroom, an isolated teen with lip rings and a modest MySpace following, and then an eighteen-year-old wannabe in Hollywood surviving on 7-Eleven pizza.

My face went from a sloppily screen-printed image on a T-shirt to the covers of magazines. In an industry ravaged by change and dismissive of loud guitars and louder haircuts, we'd landed a major label deal and earned a devoted following. Something about Black Veil Brides connected with other outcasts like me, just as I always hoped it would.

The song that gave us the three-peat milestone at the Golden Gods was "In the End," an anthem written in tribute to my late grandfather. He was a World War II veteran who always believed in me, whether I was drawing pictures of Batman or singing along with *The Phantom of the Opera*. I could barely wait to tell the world this one was for him.

The 2013 Golden Gods Awards should have been a victory lap. It was not.

As we heard the famous voice of Skid Row say "Black Veil Brides," we made our way from behind the stage props and took our place in front of the cameras. When Sebastian spoke our name, the reaction was immediate. And it was not congratulatory.

The venue swelled with an incredulous cacophony of negativity, a pissed-off chorus of spite. Our band sure inspired that crowd: we united them in their hatred of us.

The year before, we'd done a song with Dee Snider of Twisted Sister, whose big hit was "We're Not Gonna Take It." Just like Dee or Sebastian or any of my heroes before me, *I* wasn't going to take it, either. I came out on stage grabbing my crotch and waving my middle finger right back at the angry faces who stared at me. Some people spat at us.

Fans who watched the show at home may think the tables out there were full of rock stars and industry types, but in reality, the floor was filled with ticket buyers who were there to see the year's headlining act, and that's about it. It's hard enough for any band who isn't Guns N' Roses or Metallica. But this crowd despised us. They were outraged.

The rest of the guys made their way to the microphone to claim our prize. I prowled the stage instead. I locked eyes with specific people in the audience, anyone who seemed particularly antagonistic toward us. I wanted my resistance, my *defiance*, to be clear.

We had always been a polarizing band. Given how divisive we were (because of our image, our music, our personalities, and every other reason people chose), we felt honor-bound to champion the true believers that long supported us with passionate strength. After all, the Golden Gods Awards were chosen by *the fans*, the ones voting online.

I grabbed the microphone. It was my turn to speak.

"Here's the thing!" I bellowed, in my best professional wrestler voice. (WWE star Chris Jericho, who hosted, later complimented my "heel turn.") "You motherfuckers should have voted for somebody [else] because Black Veil Brides won three years in a row."

"Let me say one thing!" I continued as I pointed at one particularly hateful guy. "I know that you, fat motherfucker, and you right there"—I looked at another guy—"you hate us."

I hoisted our new trophy in the air. "I'm holding a heavy as shit award. So, fuck with me right now, motherfuckers." The booing became even louder. I wasn't finished yet.

"Here's the thing!" (I must have been going for a three-peat with "thing," too.) "Black Veil Brides have a song on the radio." I glared at someone. "*You* have a fat fucking ass."

"I don't care what any of you fat, bearded motherfuckers say. Black Veil Brides won the Best Song of the Year." Even in the midst of all of the hatred coming at me and the piss and vinegar I spat right back, I didn't forget whom I most needed to salute.

My grandfather. "This one goes out to Urban Flanders."

That acceptance speech (if we can call it that) became something of a YouTube legend in certain circles. Honestly, that's fine with me. I haven't backed down from what I said.

I won't ever apologize for speaking my mind, for defending myself, or for protecting my band. We should all respect ourselves enough to stand proudly. I did, however, take to Twitter to accept responsibility for hurting anyone who struggles with body image issues related to weight. Please understand that in that moment on stage, my dam had broken.

I looked at those angry faces and saw everyone who ever ridiculed the music I liked, mocked the way I dressed, teased me about my speaking voice, or told me my dreams were impossible. I saw the scene kids back home who targeted me on message boards, the commenters who bashed "Knives and Pens" and its earnest anti-bullying message.

My quest for revenge against my enemies (real and imagined) wasn't over. As much as I'd accomplished, I still felt like that Catholic-school reject, raging against the world.

2

KISS & MAKE UP

I WAS BORN IN December 1990, but I can tell you everything about the 1988 Bengals. I'm likewise schooled in 1989's *Hot in the Shade*, the fifteenth studio album by KISS.

When I was around seven years old, shopping for CDs with my parents at the now-defunct big-box retailer Media Play, I wondered why new music didn't seem to have the same longevity as the bands my father grew up loving. Everything contemporary felt disposable and impermanent. The early to mid-nineties were filled with one-hit wonders like Crash Test Dummies, Tonic, Marcy Playground, and so many momentary hitmakers.

I gravitated more toward music from previous generations.

It was the same with sports. The Cincinnati Bengals used to go to the Super Bowl regularly. The Cincinnati Reds won the World Series the year I was born. The interest I had in the teams I grew up cheering for was predicated on past success.

So, on the most basic level, the two things that I enjoyed the most in my adolescence—music and sports—were steeped in nostalgia. I dealt entirely in nostalgia for things I couldn't have experienced. But I knew all of the facts and could put myself in the position of remembering it or even thinking that I had been there in some capacity.

Nearly every memory that I have, the genuinely vivid ones, involves performing in some way. The thing I liked about sports as a kid was that it was an opportunity for people to watch me; that was one thing that drew me to the goalie position. There's only one of you. (Of course, the *main* thing I loved about that position was getting to wear that badass mask.)

I wanted to be the world's first rock-star-professional-hockey-player-actor-comedian multi-hyphenate. I painted vivid mental pictures of myself in those roles.

From the moment I knew I wanted to be in a band, I wanted to be the front man.

It's hard for me to understand what makes someone choose to be a guitar player or a drummer instead of a singer. Don't get me wrong. I love all of the instrumentation in rock music, and I have tremendous respect for the patience, practice, talent, and ability required to learn an instrument. I get the appeal of playing drums or guitar. But when forming a band, I wanted to be the vocalist. Plus, I knew as a lyricist, I could convey a message. I would ask my mom, "Why would anyone want any other job?"

When I was three or four, I wore these Fisher-Price roller skates and insisted that my parents introduced me before I entered a room. "Ladies and gentlemen, please welcome Little Johnny Rickfield!" I liked the name "Johnny" and heard the name Rick Springfield on the radio. I added "Little" because I was small—Little Johnny Rickfield.

My mom tells me that my interest in musical theater developed via Disney cartoons like *The Lion King* and her Barbara Streisand VHS tape. When I was around five, I saw something about *The Phantom of the Opera* on television and felt immediately drawn to it. I became obsessed for a long time. I had my tonsils out when I was seven, and to cheer me up, my aunt brought a book about *Phantom* to the hospital. I loved that book.

Michael Crawford had the coolest role. He got to wear the makeup, the mask, and the cape. The lyrics conveyed the story's themes. I wanted that.

The quest was always to find a stage to perform. If the museum center is having a Christmas pageant, and four kids are going to get to dance with the snowman, I'd better be one of those kids! When my elementary school had a talent show, I sang "Music of the Night" from *Phantom*, wearing the mask and cape, of course.

I loved the theatricality of comic book superheroes. My dad introduced me to Batman with the sixties TV series that starred the late Adam West as the Caped Crusader.

I walked my neighborhood dressed as Batman even when it wasn't Halloween.

My love of Gotham City's vigilante detective led to my first musical fandom: KISS.

My dad kept a set of KISS trading cards from the seventies in the basement. Those cards were my introduction to the band. I remember wondering, "Is this Batman?"

Nope. It was Gene Simmons, aka "the Demon," bassist and co-vocalist of KISS.

My dad is a big fan of sports, music, and comics. But I don't know that he was ever as big of a KISS fan as I became. Except for the Green Bay Packers (he's originally from Wisconsin), baseball, and a few other sports-related things (including soccer, which I never got into as much), that's probably the case with most everything I discovered through him. His hints at super fandom became my *obsessions*.

It would be difficult for anyone to match the affinity I had for the things I loved. I wasn't interested in socializing with other kids. I didn't have a brother or sister. But I had VHS tapes where Gene Simmons and Paul Stanley taught me about adulthood. They put together well-structured sentences and utilized the English language in a way that encouraged me to become more intelligent. I wanted to sound like them when I spoke.

I also wanted the makeup, the huge crazy hair, and the loud guitars.

The first album I ever bought was *Revenge,* with some cash my grandfather had given me for "helping" him blacktop his backyard. *Revenge* was their first studio album with drummer Eric Singer, who'd replaced the late Eric Carr, himself the replacement for Peter Criss, aka "the Catman." It was a great time to discover KISS because by 1996 the original lineup was back together, in the makeup, on the Alive/Worldwide Tour.

I had the KISS Action Figures made by McFarlane Toys, the company started by the artist, Spawn creator, and Image Comics cofounder Todd McFarlane. His KISS figures were the successor to the classic "dolls" first made in the late seventies. The elaborate miniaturized KISS stage sets I built in my room to put on make-believe concerts included working lights I cobbled together from our Christmas decorations.

In terms of how I would conduct myself as a musician both onstage and in conversation with fans and the press, no one was more important for me than "the Starchild," Paul Stanley. I wanted to be like Gene Simmons onstage and Paul Stanley offstage.

It wasn't his makeup, his songs, or his stage presence. His live persona can be a bit silly. I have more of an affinity for it now, and I've always respected how he commands attention. (There's even a viral bootleg collection called "People, Let Me Get This Off My Chest," which compiles a bunch of his stage banter.) I certainly give him credit for creating something memorable up there, but it wasn't my favorite thing about him.

What I liked most about the KISS vocalist/guitarist is the way he carried himself in interviews. I never really identified with the womanizing or tough-talking know-it-all attitude of Gene. I was drawn to the way Paul spoke. I loved his intelligence, his fearlessness when called upon to defend his band, and his self-deprecating humor.

Musically, KISS taught me how important it is to give an audience a reason to sing along. KISS is why I later got into the Misfits and AFI. A song like "Knives and Pens" is representative of the lessons I've learned about structure and hooks. Whether the crowd identifies with my lyrics or not, the chorus is an invitation to participate.

My personality was very much shaped by Paul and, to some extent, Gene, as well. Take, for example, the parlor trick with the vocabulary I have long employed. I don't mean to say that I'm this disingenuous guy who's trying to fool everybody. Still, I've come to realize that my interest in collecting words and drawing from a deep well of language when speaking all traces back to listening to Gene and Paul on those VHS tapes.

Context is everything, and I happened to catch them at a unique point in their career. Gene and Paul were just old enough to be reflective about their past yet still young enough to be upset about the bleak look of the future for rock 'n' roll. The early nineties were a long way from their seventies heyday and their multiplatinum eighties. New KISS albums weren't selling as they had before, and their concerts weren't as well attended.

It's worth pointing out that KISS always watched the trends with acute business savvy. During the eighties, the band was sort of Paul Stanley's solo project. They locked into the hair metal thing that was happening on radio and

MTV and revived the brand after the changing lineups of the makeup years had taken their toll on KISS commercially.

Ask ten fans about the "sound" of KISS and there may be ten different answers, depending on which era of the group served as an individual's entry point to the band.

The most considerable portion of their fanbase will swear that the KISS "sound" is this particular seventies vibe. But I would argue that sonic style was as much "borrowed" as any other. There are plenty of things about their early songs that were derivative. Bands like Sweet and Slade undoubtedly influenced KISS in the old days. Even a lot of ideas they get credit for weren't necessarily original, which I know frustrates some people. (No point in denying that both Alice Cooper and the New York Dolls arrived before KISS.)

I have never criticized them for it. For me, it was beautiful. Because here was this one band that represented all these different eras all by themselves. Want their Bon Jovi record? "Hide Your Heart" on *Hot in the Shade* is practically a rewrite of "Livin' on a Prayer," replacing the story of "Tommy and Gina" with one about "Johnny and Rosa." Want their Alice In Chains record? There's *Carnival of Souls: The Final Sessions*, which I believe has the band's best lyrics. (As a six-year-old, I would sit in my bedroom and cry listening to Gene sing about the death of a friend in "Childhood's End.") There's that big commercial crossover, "I Was Made for Lovin' You," a massive hit in the days of disco.

They've worked to stay relevant for close to fifty years now and succeeded. How is that a bad thing? There's a reason why they've been so successful for so long.

My interest in sports played into my love of KISS, as well. Fans will look back fondly on a particular period of their favorite team. I don't see it any differently with KISS.

By the time I was born, original guitarist Ace Frehley (the "Spaceman") had already been succeeded by Vinnie Vincent (both in and then out of makeup), the late Mark St. John, and Bruce Kulick, who was in KISS for over a decade. Carr ("the Fox") was the drummer through the eighties. Sure, I may have liked to see this or that running back from before I was born on the field, but this player we have now is *my* running back—my era.

My views on KISS are different from other bands. I don't have the attitude that everyone is replaceable in every group. I'm just saying that for my first love in music and for that matter, pop culture, I saw the member changes the same way I saw anything else.

Gene and Paul made ridiculous statements about what KISS was and what they would achieve throughout the seventies. But the duo I encountered on my television via these VHS tapes were in this unique period. They were no longer as over the top with their pronouncements. By the nineties, the world had beaten them down enough to where they were a bit more realistic, though, of course, still not without some hubris.

And that's where my persona developed.

I wonder about "the chicken or the egg" scenario. Did I fall in love with KISS because I'm this old soul, or did they inform the world that I saw at that age more than I ever realized? Do I often come off like an older, more jaded person because of their influence, or was there always that jadedness inside of me that responded to them?

It certainly affected a lot of my life. Those were my most formative stages when it came to my areas of interest and what I wound up doing professionally as an adult. When I consider that I'm doing today what I imagined I'd be doing with my life because of those KISS VHS tapes, I'd be kind of a fool not to give credit to where that came from for me.

KISS didn't really get into the whole Tony Robbins–style self-help vibe until that era, which for whatever reason, and whether it was genuine or not, worked perfectly for me.

It instilled a drive in me for self-preservation, self-excitement, and self-discovery. I had that when I was six years old, well before most kids are teased. A six-year-old may feel ignored or made fun of a little bit, but it's really not until a kid gets older that people like me start to suffer the perpetual hell of being the "weird person" somewhere.

The hell they had received from critics throughout their career shaped the attitude projected by KISS. It's not for me to evaluate their entire rationale behind it, but I suspect it was a way of giving those affirmations to themselves as much as to their fans.

Whatever the motives were, it worked. It was crucial to me. The simple ideas that I liked cool things, that the things that made me who I am are valid, and that it doesn't matter if other people don't like (or don't understand) what I enjoy or who I am.

3

AMY & CHRIS

I DON'T SUBSCRIBE TO the theory that a person has to be "special" or gifted to be able to do what I do for a living. I'm not some otherworldly being that was dropped from the sky to rock planet Earth. Like Gene and Paul, I believe in dedication, hard work, and drive.

I started planning everything I'm doing when I was eight. None of this was by accident. I had to wait to be old enough to do most of this stuff, but I already had the plan.

Some people figure they don't have to get their lives together till they're thirty. I always think, "Why weren't you getting your life together a long time ago?"

When I was a guest on Kevin Smith's *Fatman On Batman* podcast in early 2018, the *Clerks* and *Mallrats* filmmaker delivered a massive compliment. "You are incredibly well-heeled. You are a credit to your parents," he said. "That's something I remember, in my childhood, I'd hear and be like, 'What does that mean?' But as an adult [and] a parent, whenever I meet somebody [like you], I'm like, 'Man, somebody raised you right.'"

I told him that my parents are my best friends and that they always have been.

"Did you say they were your best friends?" His eyes widened. He said he might cry.

My mom and dad must own more Black Veil Brides and Andy Black merch than anyone else. They were at all of the shows in the early days, and they still come when they can.

My parents never made me feel like I couldn't accomplish something simply because I was "just a kid." For as long as I can remember, both of them spoke to me like I was an adult. I'm not passing judgment on other childrearing styles, but I often encounter people who must have been taught early on that they weren't capable of success.

As a middle-class family in Southern Ohio, we didn't have a lot of money when I was growing up, but I wasn't interested in expensive things, anyway. I couldn't afford to have the latest Air Jordans. I wanted KISS action figures, acrylic paint pens, and hockey pads. As a teenager, I wanted blank T-shirts to paint all over before I wore them.

My mom, Amy, taught me the value of kindness over wealth. I see it in her everyday interactions with people. In her work, she helps sick kids and their families.

I talk to her every day. We have a real closeness intellectually and emotionally. I credit her with my comedic sensibilities, too. We laugh at the same things.

When I was little, my mom was a manager at a family-owned restaurant chain. After the location closed, she went to work at Cincinnati Children's Hospital Medical Center, where she was the manager of a hospital coffee shop called "the Rainbow Room."

The hospital recognized her skillset was much broader than food service and moved her over to the volunteer services department. She now heads a major department at the Children's Hospital. During her time there, she earned a degree online. Her life is entirely different now than it was when I was a kid, and I find that incredible. She had clearly defined values, a plan for where she saw herself, and she did the work to arrive there.

Most days, I wouldn't see my mom again after she dropped me at school till the late evening when she'd get home from the diner. If I were already in bed, she'd come in and kiss my forehead. She often smelled like French fries. To this day, the familiar scent of fries on clothing soothes me the way a perfume might comfort someone else.

I spent most of my time with my father, Chris. Black Veil Brides fans are well acquainted with him via his very active social media presence, always in support of my endeavors.

In the early eighties, long before I was born, my dad sang in local bands. One of them became a regional touring outfit. They even opened for the original Glenn Danzig–led incarnation of the Misfits at the world-famous rock, punk, and hardcore club, CBGB, in Manhattan's East Village. They supported Social Distortion at one point, too.

After his last band broke up, my dad did the responsible thing, which was to make use of his education and earn enough to provide for our family. He had a couple of degrees already and went back to get his master's in Human Resource Development in 1994. He's worked in labor relations for the local government for most of his professional life.

I liked hanging out with my dad. My social interaction was kind of covered. I didn't feel like I needed friends. My parents weren't very social and didn't hang out with a lot of people. I can probably count on one hand the number of close friends my dad had when I was a kid. He tired of people quickly and had a habit of short-lived friendships.

I would have never had any of the opportunities I've had were it not for my dad's relentless and tireless drive to ensure I could have anything I wanted from life.

I can only imagine there was significant pressure on my parents financially, but that was never exhibited to me. While they spoke to me like I was an adult, they never burdened me with grown-up problems. They wanted me to dream big. They wanted me to aspire beyond the west side of Cincinnati. They made sure I never felt limited by any obstacle.

I loved my childhood with my family. They were never the issue. The problems arose when I encountered my peers. I just thought of them as, you know, children. Even at age eight, I'd tell my mom, "Wow, kids are dumb." I felt like I was already forty-five years old.

I was only ever really around my grandparents, aunts, older cousins, and my mom and dad. I wasn't used to talking with people my age. It was difficult enough to pay attention to my schoolwork, so the idea of making a bunch of pals seemed impossible anyway. The chip on my shoulder toward the other kids came from a lack of tolerance for being "childish," which came from a lack of experience with it or understanding of it.

Remember, everything I liked was old. The music I loved was long past relevancy. I can vividly recall several times when I said KISS was my favorite thing to listen to, and the reaction was always, "Oh, Kiss 107.1?" (That was our local pop radio station.)

I was already a bit of a self-serious melancholy loner, so those conversations quickly frustrated me, and I'd shut down. "Whatever, I'll watch my KISS tapes alone."

Even the Batman I first fell in love with was more of an outsider than Bruce Wayne. For a time in the early nineties in the comics, as a broken back sidelined the original Caped Crusader, a character named Jean-Paul Valley (aka Azrael) took up the mantle. He was affiliated with a group of assassins created by the Sacred Order of Saint Dumas.

I have a tattoo on my arm of the Azrael Batman. (As Smith joked, "Even the creator of Jean-Paul Valley doesn't have him tattooed on his body.") My dad has several Batman tattoos, as do I. He took me to get my favorite hero put on me when I was sixteen. He got one inked in the same place on *his* arm, too, albeit a more traditional Batman.

Like I told Kevin, my parents have always been my best friends. I didn't need to hang out with people my age because I had my life at home. I feel genuinely awful for anyone whose mom or dad ditched their parental duties altogether, were abusive, passed away, or simply weren't there for them emotionally. The support from my family was my armor out in the world. I never had to complain that "I just wish my parents were behind me."

I don't think anything I accomplished surprised them. It can be a blessing and a curse because we all want our folks to be impressed with what we do. (They have always been proud of me, but they haven't ever been *astonished* by me.) I'd imagine most adults patronizingly dismiss the grand designs of the average seven-year-old.

My mom and dad always took me at my word.

4

GHOSTS & GRAVEYARDS

Like so many things I love, Tim Burton's *Batman* movie premiered before I was born, (albeit only by a year). Burton took a page from some of the more cerebral comics that emphasized the idea of Bruce Wayne as the ultimate outsider. The Jean-Paul Valley incarnation of Batman was even more of an outcast, as he fought common street criminals, the vicious Bane, and finally, the original Batman himself.

The sweeping themes of dedication to principle and justice amidst the darkness in Batman stories shared much in common with the greatest heavy metal bands. Black Sabbath, Judas Priest, and Iron Maiden are among those who spun epic tales of tragedy and heroism while dressed as characters from the pages of pulp literature.

KISS has appeared in several comics, beginning in 1977. The following year KISS even starred in a made-for-TV-movie, *KISS Meets the Phantom of the Park*, where they used superpowers to battle an evil inventor at Six Flags Magic Mountain. (It's as awesomely bad as it sounds.) With his leather wings and penchant for spitting fire and blood, the "Demon" of KISS wouldn't look out of place taking down a Gotham City bank.

Gotham may be a work of fiction, but there are corners of the world with similar sensibilities. An International Gothic Association Conference takes place in Manchester, England; visiting a site like Salford Cathedral, there is an excellent insight into how groups from Joy Division to The Smiths draped their music in morose imagery. The dense wintery forests of Norway might explain some of the most famous black metal music.

The dark angels, savage beasts, mysterious cloaked figures, and crucified characters adorning Black Veil Brides album covers and T-shirts may not "feel" like the Midwest at first glance. My hometown wasn't exactly Oslo, let alone Gotham City. Yet even with its small-city charm and American heartland locale, Cincinnati has a surprisingly grim and morbid underbelly comprised of a mixture of verifiable facts, local legends, and tall tales.

There are areas with cryptic histories of hauntings and spooky occurrences, giving them a gothic ambiance. Call it coincidence, call it predestination, but there's certainly something to be said for the connection between the atmosphere of these places and the types of music, imagery, and even fashion that's long held my fascination.

It isn't too desolate where my parents are now, mostly just houses and a few fast-food restaurants. But Western Hills, where I first lived, grows sadder looking each year.

Generally speaking, the west side of Cincinnati is really depressing. It's as dead as a place can be. Even as recently as when I was growing up, there were local businesses, bright colors. It felt like people lived there. Much of it is just empty, impoverished, and gray. Nothing new ever seems to open on the west side. Nothing fun happens there. Economic recession and wealth inequality have decimated the place.

Of course, some neighborhoods are better than others. There are grocery stores, Chipotle, and that sort of thing. But mostly the area is odd and empty. It all feels ghostly.

Infamous 1960s cult leader Charles Manson was born in Cincinnati and died in a California prison. (Brian Warner, whose stage name is an amalgamation of fifties film star Marilyn Monroe and "Manson Family" mastermind Charles, was born in Canton, Ohio.)

The Dunham Recreation Center sits a few miles west of downtown Cincinnati. Years before the preschool, archery classes, golf courses, senior activities, baseball games, theater performances, a swimming pool, and other programs, the Center was Dunham Hospital, a branch of the Cincinnati Hospital used to quarantine tuberculosis patients.

A city ordinance in 1816 called for the creation of an "Isolation Hospital" or "Pest-house" for smallpox patients in hopes of protecting other patients from infection. There were different locations established for the treatment of smallpox. In 1873 the city purchased a fifty-three-acre farm and set up the Branch Hospital for Contagious Diseases.

Several structures were built there over the years. By 1920 the hospital could house as many as 450 patients. There was separate lodging for doctors and nurses, a laundry area, an occupational therapy building, a preventorium for patients' children, and a school for the kids to take classes. The sanatorium was renamed Dunham Hospital in 1945, after tuberculosis researcher Dr. Henry Kennon Dunham. By 1967, about twenty years after a cure was found, the number of patients there fell to about two hundred.

The hospital was finally closed in 1971. Many of the buildings, including the main hospital, were demolished when it was transformed into a rec center. Other buildings, like the nurse's dormitory, were simply refurbished. A community theater group has used the occupational therapy building since 1980, which was converted into an auditorium. The laundry facility is now a parking garage. The school is an arts center.

When the notorious "Pest House" was up and running, workers used a series of underground tunnels to travel from building to building. Those tunnels remain today.

The bodies of the dead had to go somewhere. There's a twenty-five-acre cemetery just up Guerley Road in Price Hill, a Potter's Field, where Hamilton County's impoverished, cast aside, and forgotten were buried. Between 1849 and 1981, as many as ten thousand were laid to rest there, including Civil War veterans and many from the "Pest House," which controlled Potter's Field from 1879 till 1912. The Dunham

Hospital dead were buried quickly and often without funerals. Thousands of the graves there remain unmarked.

Naturally, the entire area that was once Dunham Hospital and its nearby burial grounds are considered "haunted" by many locals and curious seekers of the strange and paranormal. Local legend contends that Potter's Field was also a burial ground for those deemed to be too "evil" to receive a Christian burial in consecrated ground.

The haunted tunnels hidden beneath Dunham Recreation Center and its surrounding buildings are where I spent a lot of my childhood—like, an *excessive* amount of my time. Take a look at the creepy photographs found on websites about the area's famous hauntings. The locations in every photo are places where little Andy Biersack played.

I attended preschool, day camps, dance classes, cooking classes, golf lessons, and baseball games, all in one of the most famous "haunted" abandoned hospitals in the United States or on the land surrounding it, which included that extra creepy cemetery.

As a kid, I had no idea it was considered haunted or even scary. I hadn't heard its history, but I found it to be awful and horrifying nonetheless. We were all terrified exploring those grounds; every hallway, each corridor, seemed scary and dark.

On any given activity-filled day, mean older kids would force the younger ones to play the game where a person holding a lit candle repeats the name "Bloody Mary" into a mirror. It's supposed to summon an evil spirit. (A variation of "Bloody Mary" found its way into the 1992 horror movie classic *Candyman*, based on Clive Barker's *The Forbidden*.)

Of course, none of us knew that the former Dunham Hospital had been home to so much more suffering and death than our little minds could have possibly imagined.

The auditorium they made out of the old occupational therapy building remains among the more frightening places I've ever visited. They'd show us the *Ernest* movies, starring Jim Varney, on VHS in there. That "theater" was just a fearsome cave. I can't say I "experienced" anything really, but I always found it to be grim and creepy.

There's also the Dent Schoolhouse, a red brick building built in 1894 and maintained as a school until the fifties. Local legend has it that the bodies of several missing students were discovered in the school's basement, sealed in barrels and hidden behind walls. The school janitor was the only suspect. He evaded capture, disappearing into myth.

There are no historical documents to support this story, although the FAQ section on the Dent Schoolhouse website says every bit is real. The Dent Schoolhouse is a long-running Halloween haunted house attraction with costumed actors and the whole bit.

Morbid and chilling occurrences where I grew up stretched beyond ghost stories, too.

Near Cincinnati/Northern Kentucky International Airport (CVG), there's a road winding down a mountainside that spits out at the bottom along the Ohio River. A rickety old boat ferries cars across the river and to the bottom of the hills leading up into Delhi. It's a maze of hills and shanty homes in every direction as far as the eye can see.

There are no streetlights. At night everything is black. The only illumination is whatever lights are coming from the huts and houses that line the narrow mountain roads. At the top of the mountain is quiet middle-class suburbia overlooking the Ohio River. There's something about the hills and the woods in Delhi that feels supernaturally odd.

Six people died in "hill hopping" accidents during the year leading up to my tenth birthday. It's a type of adrenaline rush joyriding where kids drive super fast up a steep hill and then "fly" for a few seconds. The site of one deadly crash in Delhi, Ohio, has since been leveled; a teenager, who'd just gotten her license three days before, took a bunch of friends hill hopping in her mom's Jeep. Two thirteen-year-old girls died.

I took my Geo Metro down that scary-as-hell road one evening and got that dual feeling of terror and ecstasy that hill hoppers describe even at a mere thirty miles per hour. I knew three or four people whose older brothers or sisters had died while hill hopping.

There are parallels to be found with the things I love in pop culture. The dark romance of devil-may-care thrill rides is all over the teenage vampire classic *The Lost Boys*. So many of the bands I adored growing up dealt in imagery cloaked in blood and death.

It often surprises people to learn that the cryptic and macabre aesthetics I wield in my art (like many of the musicians and filmmakers I love) once chilled me to the bone.

Long before I starred in *American Satan*, named songs things like "Coffin," or had discovered the Misfits, I lived with crushing anxiety.

It was just as described in "Fear of the Dark," the Grammy-nominated early nineties Iron Maiden anthem from the album of the same name:

"Fear of the dark

Fear of the dark

I have a constant fear that something's always near."

5

DEATH & BASEBALL

IN ONE SCENE IN the comic book movie classic *The Crow*, crime boss Top Dollar admires a snow globe with a tiny cemetery inside of it. "Dad gave this to me. Fifth birthday," he explains. "He said, 'Childhood's over the moment you know you're gonna die.'"

I was five the day my dad and I saw a man drop dead in front of us.

It was April 1, 1996, a little less than two years after *The Crow* hit theaters. My father would come up with reasons, like doctor visits, to get me out of school to go to baseball games. I remember walking out once and a teacher saying, "Have fun at Opening Day!" It was practically a holiday in Cincinnati, anyway. Baseball is a huge deal.

On this particular Opening Day, some 44,000 people were there with us at Riverfront Stadium to see the Cincinnati Reds play the Montreal Expos. We went to a lot of games, so we'd get the cheap seats. The hard-painted metal of the chairs was hot from the sun.

The first pitch from the Reds' new addition, Pete Schourek, went straight down the middle of the plate. But the umpire was oddly silent. As we looked on from the stands (and as people watched on TV at home), veteran umpire John Patrick McSherry clutched his chest, stumbled toward the medics, then collapsed face-first to the ground.

McSherry had umpired in the World Series twice before I was born. He was a big guy, which wasn't uncommon for umpires back then. He died of a massive heart attack.

It didn't register as "scary" to me at first. It was just very confusing.

They had everyone exit the stadium and promised to reschedule the game. I remember asking my dad, "That isn't going to happen again, right?"

It was so strange to see this person die several hundred feet away from me. It wasn't a violent death. He wasn't a friend or a loved one. What eventually troubled me was the *finality* of it. "That man is dead and gone, and he's never going to come back."

I suppose if there were any single event that could have triggered the constant and irrational fear I developed over the next several months, it would certainly be that.

I became afraid that dark and powerful forces would kill me. I had trouble sleeping with the lights off. At six years old, I was still crawling into bed with my parents. I was convinced a horrific doom awaited me. I couldn't walk down a hallway at school without wondering what monster, apparition, or demon was waiting around every corner.

Mind you, I was never thinking about murder. I didn't have vivid, violent imagery in my head. I wasn't worried about getting stabbed or bleeding everywhere. No, I didn't believe I'd collapse from a heart attack on the baseball field. There wasn't any specificity to my fear, which was part of what made it so difficult to overcome.

It was more the idea that "something" could get me. The towering, cloaked figure on the cover of *Wretched and Divine* is the type of entity I feared might be lurking nearby.

A quick image, like the trailer for a *Halloween* movie flashing by, was all it would take to scare me half to death. I found myself engaging in obsessive, ritualistic, compulsive behaviors, like flushing a certain number of times in a row, to "ensure" my safety.

At times this voice in my head would vividly detail for me all of the ways my life could suddenly end. "You could jump out of this car. You could fall down a well." It was particularly bad whenever my dad and I would walk across the bridge over the Ohio River to get to sports events in downtown Cincinnati. He'd hold my hand as we crossed while my "friend" inside my head would tell me how I could easily leap off.

It confirmed something I had already suspected, which was that I could hurt myself. I didn't want to, at all, but I knew that I *could*. I could throw myself over. I could fall.

I thought about things I could do to myself and things that could happen to me. I was equally terrified of outside forces and a lack of self-control, though to this day I've never done anything to hurt myself intentionally. I wanted to be a carefree kid. But I was full of cares and burdened by unwanted thoughts of certain and decisive death.

When I found KISS and later discovered bands like AFI and The Misfits, something turned in me. I loved the theatricality of it all. It struck a chord, like *Phantom*. I never felt like Gene Simmons was going to murder me. The Misfits hired the late Basil Gogos (who died in 2017) to create the cover for their second "Resurrection Era" album, 1999's *Famous Monsters*. Gogos was responsible for many incredible illustrations in *Famous Monsters of Filmland* magazine. When I saw that album cover, I fell in love with the dark.

The Misfits was a beacon for me. They looked like "monsters," but they were accessible fiends. It was a type of horror with just enough camp to be inviting versus terrifying, a joyous celebration of the darkness. The ghostly white face paint, black makeup beneath the eyes, and "devilock" hairstyles made it all feel like Halloween. Like Batman, the Misfits twisted fear into a righteous weapon. These four guys turned it into outsider *fun*.

Bruce Wayne was a lonely orphan afraid of bats. He took his greatest fear and remade it as his symbol to strike fear into the hearts of criminals and inspire hope for Gotham City. What's cooler than a guy who is afraid of bats becoming Batman?

I'm generally not a dark person. I don't read a lot about mass murderers or serial killers. I don't paint my walls black. I don't hang out at the Museum of Death (though I did take the woman who became my wife there on one of our first dates).

I'm drawn to these aesthetics (and I enjoy the night), but I don't dwell in negativity.

The dark and macabre theatricality of the Misfits and the similar bands I discovered helped me recognize, confront, and ultimately embrace my fears. This fantastical fairy-tale stuff like ghosts, zombies, vampires, haunted houses, I think it exists to help us process our mortality. (The *reality* of death is much grimmer because it's mundane.)

As I immersed myself further, I felt like I could move forward without the limitations of my fears. I still wasn't very social, but I was more content in my relative solitude.

I *did* love the idea of entertaining people. I wasn't fond of talking with classmates, but on the other hand, I was happy to tell a great joke. "You don't want to get to know me or hang out with me, but I bet I can dazzle you." I've always had that feeling inside of me. I was best at making adults laugh, which was fine since they were my target audience.

I knew these kids wouldn't care about me the rest of the day in class, but I felt like if I participated in the school talent shows, in my *Phantom of the Opera* cape and mask singing "The Music of the Night," I'd have some recognition for that moment. I don't know if that was entirely effective, but I do know that I made an impression. I craved that.

When other elementary school kids would ask me what I liked, I'd say, "KISS and W.A.S.P." As I mentioned earlier, they all seemed to be into pop music. Eventually, I grew tired of those conversations and retreated to drawing pictures by myself.

I never really became social with people until I made my first real friend, Kenny. We became pals in third grade. He seemed to be a loner, too. I was probably a bit patronizing since I thought of myself as an "adult" and subsequently saw him more like a little brother than a peer. (I worshipped Batman, so I took it upon myself to stand up for him as a self-appointed superhero. The same kids made fun of us both.) Kenny and I bonded over rock bands. He loved Metallica the same way that I loved KISS. I'd show him my KISS VHS tapes and he'd introduce me to Metallica videos.

The music that refashioned the subjects of my anxiety into new passions had also helped me make a friend. I was now armed with a *healthy* obsession with the darkness.

It wasn't my adversary any longer. It became my ally.

BLOOD & ICE

Like the *Famous Monsters* album cover, I found the icy cool of a hockey goalie's mask captivating. I don't recall where I first saw one, exactly, but I remember the feeling it gave me. The killer look of Jason in the *Friday the 13th* series is one solid reference point. It gave me the same feelings of empowerment as the Misfits and everything else I had come to admire. There's just something special about that iconography of the dark.

I wanted to wear that mask. So I decided to get into hockey.

Cincinnati is primarily a football town. It's no secret how much I love my Bengals (*Who Dey!*). As a bigger kid, I would have played one of the less glamorous positions on the field, and as we've established, I'm a lead singer type. I aspired toward something more "special." Of course, sports like hockey and lacrosse can be pretty cost-prohibitive for working families, especially in places like Cincinnati. The monetary burden only increases as the player develops more skills, the more competitive he or she becomes, and the more out-of-state tournaments and other costly adventures there are.

But my dad always did everything he could to make anything I wanted happen, so he tore up the carpet in our basement to create an area for me to practice. Then he took me to Play It Again Sports, a chain of second-hand equipment stores, to get me as much used gear as he could afford. I created this project for the three of us.

We would become a hockey family.

My dad even cofounded a team with another parent. They named us the Cincinnati Swords, after an American Hockey League team that was around in the early seventies.

As soon as I got on the ice, I took to it with relative ease. I was able to go forward just fine. Still, even more importantly, I became exceptionally good at skating backward, which is critical for playing goalie as that is the direction in which you're skating most of the game. You head out to cut off the angle of the shooter and then work your way back toward the net. It's about learning the angles and developing an understanding of where the net is in relation to your position at all times peripherally. I learned how to do figure eights backward. I could cross my legs, going backward. I could do everything. It's not an easy skill to develop, but for whatever reason, it clicked for me.

I was so excited about it early on that I wanted to share it with my dad. I wanted to teach him how to skate backward too. We went to a park near our house, and in my youthful exuberance, I was rollerblading much too fast for him to be a competent instructor. He did his best to keep up with me but ended up crashing down onto the pavement.

Unfortunately, he stuck out his hand to brace his fall and broke a finger. It was a nasty break, splitting his knuckle and forcing the bone out through the skin. At the emergency room, the doctors took out what looked like a long sewing needle with a ball on the end of it. They stuck it through his finger to the very top to hold his knuckle in place.

It was supposed to stay in there for a month or so for his finger to heal correctly. About three days later, we were in his car (I believe it was the eggplant-colored Geo Metro that later became mine), and he reached under his seat to grab something, inadvertently using the hand with the healing finger. He crushed the needle deep into the base of his hand to where the ball was now touching the inside of his hand instead of sticking out of the tip of his finger like it should've been.

After we got home, he somehow managed to pull it out, which turned his finger into a geyser of blood. I remember how distressed my mother was as we watched that blood shoot out all over the kitchen. In the process of yanking it out he tore some tendons and ruined the finger for good. He's saddled with a dead finger ever since.

He just needed to keep his hand still for about two weeks for it to heal correctly. Believe me, I get it. I'm just as stubborn as my dad. As much as he was just instinctively reaching with the same hand he'd used to break his fall, there was also a big part of him that was consciously thinking, "I can reach under here and grab this thing!" We both will do whatever it takes to make something go the way we think it "should" go. As I've gotten older, I've worked to curb that attitude within myself. It can be frustrating.

My dad inspired my desire to be great at whatever I pursued. If we were going in, we were going all the way. He's apologized to me for the sternness he sometimes conveyed. He expected me to achieve a minimum level of excellence.

I was mostly into the theatricality of hockey. I romanticized the idea of presenting this masked character to the world. I was more enamored with the "costume" than the sport itself. I enjoyed playing, but the pads and the color schemes were intriguing for me. To have a chance to dress up as the goalie was like landing a role in a play. The strategy was not exciting.

We weren't at the same economic level as most of the families with kids who played hockey, so I'm sure my dad had a chip on his shoulder about that to some extent, too. Naturally, the father of the kid in the used gear wants his kid to be better than the ones with the expensive equipment. And I was, which none of those families liked.

The parents of these kids were among the more aggressive human beings I've ever encountered. They heckled, they threw things, and they even belittled their kids.

When parents put that much money into a sport, many of them are hoping for a significant return on investment, like a Division I college scholarship or a ticket to the National Hockey League, because that's the level of ego involved. Everyone is hoping his or her kid is the next Wayne Gretzky or Sidney Crosby or Jack Campbell.

I realize not every parent puts their kid in sports looking for a lottery ticket, but I don't see any real benefits. I used to believe sports taught me to be "tough," but honestly, I think I would have turned out the same without them. Building something with my dad was what was important. I didn't have to put on a costume and have people scream at me to share something with him. (Yes, I realize I'm still dressing in costumes and getting yelled at.) We could have just as easily built a boat or worked on a classic car, either of which would have required a lot of time and money too.

As children, we want to be active, become good at something, kick a ball around. But I don't agree with the almost political argument that youth sports "build character." I don't think any of us know that for sure. It seems to be more of an excuse to live vicariously through our kids. I'll never be an NFL player, but perhaps if my wife and I have a child someday we can get all of the gear and make our kid look super cool. If our little one excels at a sport, I can declare to the world, "Hey, mini-me is great! That person who shares so much of my genetic makeup is good at this sport!"

As for me and my teammates, none of us went to the NHL because we were kids playing in-line hockey in the summer in Cincinnati. The kids at my school weren't really into hockey, which meant that even with sports I'd chosen something relatively alienating.

One day our new gym teacher decided we'd spend the class playing street hockey. I don't think I ever took a gym class more seriously than I did that day. It was finally my chance to be the best at some activity and show up all of the kids that ignored me, made fun of me, or whom I thought saw me as less than them. I way overdid it.

I ran all over the place shooting the puck too hard. I must have looked ridiculous. Trying too hard only made me seem like I had no idea what I was doing. I overthought it as my "moment" to do something great and completely ruined it.

I did try to make friends with the kids on my team. We shared hockey as an interest but little else, and I still wasn't skilled at socializing. I couldn't seem to get out of my way with them, either. One time we shot airsoft guns in the hockey locker room. It was a tightly enclosed space, and one of my shots bounced off the wall and hit another kid in the cheek. I was too embarrassed to confess that it had been me, so I lied about it.

Another time, one of my teammates rode with my dad and me to a game. I made a mixtape for the drive. He was into Eminem. His exposure to rock music didn't extend much beyond whichever Blink-182 songs were on the radio. Dio's "Rainbow in the Dark" was my favorite song at the time. I loved singing it in my bedroom! It's so dramatic. It's like a show tune. It could have been in the *Phantom of the*

Opera. It was one of the many tracks I treasured on the *Beast of Dio* CD I owned. So this mixtape I put together had Dio, AC/DC, and of course, KISS. The kid who'd come along with us was friendly enough. Here's someone my age, and in a few short minutes, I put this awkward distance between us. He couldn't relate to someone so obsessed with all of this old heavy metal.

Playing sports was the first time I faced people being *genuinely* mean to me. I experienced getting booed when I was eight years old. Adults would bang on the glass, yelling, "Hit him in the throat!" I played hockey into my teens, and by then I had long hair, wore mascara, and put Misfits stickers all over my gear. I'm sure there was part of me at the Golden Gods Awards in 2013 instantly transported back to the hockey rink.

When I was about fifteen, my dad had a falling out with the other family he'd started the Swords with, so I switched over to one of our rival teams. The Lexington Snake Eyes recruited me after watching me at a few tournaments. I'm sure at least part of the motivation in courting me was to swipe the rival team's goalie. It was like I'd been cut from the Bengals and went to play for the Pittsburgh Steelers. Once I joined the Snake Eyes, our family started making regular 160-mile round-trip drives to Northern Kentucky.

The first time I was in a tournament with the Snake Eyes, we were up against the Swords. It was another opportunity to be a showman, to demonstrate my greatness and prove that nobody should ever doubt me, let alone dismiss me. But sometimes you just don't play well, and that day I was terrible. I gave up like six goals! I couldn't seem to stop anything. I wasn't nervous or injured. I was just off. It was an absolute bummer.

Not long after that, I joined the Cincinnati Storm. During one of the last games of the season, the coach put me on the bench. I had started to lose interest in hockey, yet I resented getting replaced by another goalie in the middle of the game—and so close to the local championship, no less. I recognized right away that I didn't have the fortitude to stomach benching, and if this was going to be a reality going forward, I was over it. In the locker rooms afterward, I changed out of my uniform with a distinct feeling in my stomach that I'd played my last hockey game.

My dad and I never had a conversation about my decision. He just knew. He could sense my disappointment. After the game, he drove us to the Guitar Center around the corner from the rink in a shopping area called the Tri-County Commons.

I'm so grateful my dad had the presence of mind to mark the occasion with something big. It was a clearly defined turning point as I left behind hockey and fully embraced music. We looked around inside Guitar Center without a single word between us about sports. My dad helped me choose an inexpensive bass guitar and a modest PA system with speakers. It was at that moment that I began to feel I was a bona fide musician.

I've come to understand how much I was attracted to the romanticism of loneliness. The things I loved and the person I wanted to be certainly did set me apart and were cause for uncomfortable social interactions more than once. But it was, of course, much grander to cast me as the tormented and misunderstood artist than to be someone nobody would expect anything from or remember. If I was hated, if that was in the cards for me, that was fine. But I would not abide being ignored. Irrelevance was never an option. I was committed to making my mark.

Hockey was now another thing in my rearview mirror. It was a false start as frustrating and pointless as school, an obstacle in the path toward my eventual destination rather than a stepping-stone or building block. My journey from where I began to where I am was driven so much by that constant feeling that if I hone my skills, if I'm undeniably great at something, I don't need to answer to anybody but myself. I can continue to improve and become great at whatever I do, and that will be enough. Hockey wasn't working out how I wanted it? Fine. I would put my complete focus on music, full stop.

I put everything into planning for the career in music I wanted to have. I spent countless hours scribbling in note-books, sketching out ideas for artwork and the stage dressing.

The support my parents gave me in pursuit of my dreams never wavered.

It never occurred to me that I missed out on anything as an only child until the past couple of years. I didn't have anyone to talk to that was close to my age at home. I honestly thought of myself as another adult.

I used to say things to my mom like, "Oh, I hate little kids." How obnoxious and crappy is that? People would laugh at that. "Oh, what a funny kid." But I just didn't know better.

I have cousins I enjoyed hanging out with, though most of them were older than me. I wouldn't give the time of day to the younger ones. I assumed they were stupid. They were *kids*. The abiding belief that I knew more than everybody else ultimately isolated me. I could have had more friends. I could've been more social. But the more I fell into this role that I liked of the sort of disenfranchised person that nobody understands, the easier it was for me to dismiss any kids who would've been kind to me.

If I had been less particular, I probably could've had a larger group of friends. But, in my mind, I needed people around me who would want to talk to me about all of the things I loved. I mean, I had "strong" opinions on politics when I was eight years old. It created a sort of arrested development in me. While I was eloquent and seemed like I knew a lot, I didn't have a whole lot I would talk about with other people who were my age.

There wasn't a horrible incident that happened to force me to grow up too fast. We often hear about unfortunate situations where someone has to help raise their brother or sister, or worse, care for their parents too early. Unexpected illness or death, divorce, unemployment, several factors can cause it. I didn't *have* to act like an adult at such a young age. I just wanted to.

I liked that my parents spoke to me in a way that didn't make me feel like a kid. They were never patronizing or condescending. But it made it harder to talk to people because the only things I had opinions about were sort of "adult" topics of conversation. As soon as I was able to wrap my head around life's more significant questions, for example, I was able to have honest and frank conversations about religion with my parents.

A childhood like mine generally ends with, "and that's why I stayed home my entire life," but in my case, I moved away from home almost immediately to follow this dream I had. I don't know that I was fully equipped with the armor of life experience a person needs.

And I had discarded any type of religious indoctrination well before then.

7

GOD & GORE

IT'S EASY TO UNDERSTAND the correlation between religion and horror. Both deal with death, blood, and darkness. There are immortality and murder throughout religious texts.

When I was very young, we rarely went to church. We didn't say grace at the dinner table. There wasn't much of a religious presence in my home.

My dad would sometimes go through phases where he'd be obsessed with a particular thing (much as I do now as an adult). He'd find something new and immerse himself in it. I was in second grade when he randomly drove us to a Christian bookstore one day. It was before Catholic school and before any religious conversations in my house.

He told me we were there so he could buy a necklace with a cross on it. I said, "What? You mean like Peter Criss?" He got a little bit frustrated with his smartass son's joke. He kind of half-assed a response about God, but I didn't hear any conviction behind it.

I know it was complicated for him because both of his parents stayed in the church throughout his entire life. They were true believers. It was a big part of his upbringing. So he was conflicted as a thirty-something father, trying to figure out where his head and heart were at concerning religious faith. What kind of theology did he want to teach his son?

At the time, it just gave me the creeps. I couldn't wrap my head around his journey.

We did go to mass with my grandparents every Christmas, and my grandparents were all about it. We moved into a nicer house in Delhi Township, my grandparents' heavily Roman Catholic neighborhood, and I enrolled in St. Dominic's elementary, the Catholic school my mother had gone to growing up. I was there from third till fifth grade.

Anyone who listens to the music I've made knows how much the artifice, pageantry, ceremony, and iconography of Catholicism appeals to my artistic sensibilities. I don't know if that was something put in me, or if that was always inherent with me.

I was immediately taken with the gruesome, shockingly violent imagery I encountered at St. Dominic. I mean, look at the Stations of the Cross, which depict Jesus Christ on the day of his crucifixion, to say nothing of the church's history with colonialism, the Crusades, and the patriarchy. It isn't limited to Catholicism, and there are certainly believers and theologians who cast Jesus as a liberator and champion of the oppressed. But there's no denying that when walking into many churches, we are confronted by numerous brutal pictures of death and pain, which can be equally fascinating and frightening for children.

I became enamored with all of the stories from the Bible. These are stories held up by millions of people as literal fact. These tales and traditions are revered and celebrated.

As a child, seeing people worshipping the glory of it all, I found all of it enchanting. At first, I was a firm believer in everything that came along with my understanding of Catholicism. Or so I thought. In retrospect, I'm not sure any little kid truly believes or disbelieves in any religion. At school, I quickly became disappointed in the people who were supposed to be the most informed about life's biggest mysteries.

I'd be lying if I said I was an eight-year-old atheist, but I knew the information I gathered didn't add up to the answer presented to me. Even now, as an adult, with all I've absorbed from authors, comedians, artists, and friends, I have yet to make a clearly defined "choice." I haven't joined a "team" or signed a "contract." It all remains a puzzle.

Generally, there should be a complete image when all of the pieces of a puzzle are assembled. I haven't seen that. I have yet to make all of the pieces fit.

My mom has said that my critical thinking and questioning helped steer her away from the Catholic

Church, but I think she was selling herself short. It is difficult to separate her evolution from my own because everything the three of us did was so interconnected for as long as I can remember. I was about ten when she started reading about the historical Christ, about Mary Magdalene, and about women in the church. Her frustrations with the Catholic Church increased. She talked to me about it because we talked about everything. Those conversations sparked something. It helped me question all of it, too.

Why *did* women have such limited roles? Why couldn't my grandmother be more involved after going to church every week for her entire life? That was the original thread that tugged at the whole coat of religion I had tried to put on before the whole thing unraveled.

The level of cynicism and even anger I sensed from the school's faculty just raised more questions. The more detached I felt from the staff and curriculum, the more I acted out.

I spiked my hair up. I discovered Alkaline Trio, whose lyrics heavily questioned religion. Records like *From Here to Infirmary* were full of themes of questioning and skepticism.

They said I wasn't Catholic school material, and the school officials worked hard to make my parents feel guilty as if they'd somehow failed because their son had questions.

By sixth grade, I was back in the public school system at Delhi Middle School.

Over the years, I've seen a lot of speculation about the meaning behind the lyrics to the song "Sweet Blasphemy" from the first Black Veil Brides album. While on the surface it certainly speaks about isolation and being made to feel strange or "evil" for thinking outside of the orthodoxy, it's often debated as to what exactly it says about Catholicism.

The lessons from my Catholic upbringing were varied. The practicing Catholics in my family were open-minded, kind, loving, and accepting. On the other hand, the teachers and clergy from the church itself were quite often the opposite. Getting kicked out of Catholic school led me down a path of frustration. How could those meant to be the "vessel" for God on Earth be so unkind and exclusionary? The resentment inside of me, combined with my deep interest in religious iconography and history as well as my love and respect for the family members who are devout worshippers, resulted in a mountain of inner turmoil and conflict that came out in the lyrics to "Sweet Blasphemy."

Challenging theological ideas, working through the concepts, trying to understand the meaning behind all of it, if that's "blasphemy," then I had resigned myself to the label of "blasphemous." But the song was *never* anti-Jesus Christ or even anti-religion. It is anti-exclusion. It's against the idea of faith as a weapon against those who don't share it.

I believe both of my parents have some religious faith to this day, but they certainly didn't condone the attitude the elementary school staff took toward me. I have tremendous respect for people who choose to believe as well as people who choose not to believe. I most certainly revere my grandparents and appreciate the steadfast faith they maintain.

The song should inspire people, regardless of their religious or spiritual viewpoints or lack thereof. That was the intention. Joy shouldn't be only for a "chosen" few. Hope is for everyone. There is no religion or way of thinking anyone should see as the *only* light in the darkness. As I later wrote in "Faithless" from the 2014 album:

"Even when I fall down to my knees
I never say a prayer I don't believe
And I don't want to look up to the Son
But I will never be the faithless one."

8

URBAN & ANNE

MY LATE GRANDFATHER SERVED in the Air Force during World War II. Urban Phalem Flanders was born in Hartford, Connecticut, on July 12, 1923, and grew up in nearby Windsor Locks. He was married to my grandmother, Anna Flanders (née Kock), for fifty-eight years.

He graduated from Windsor Locks High School in 1941. After World War II, he went to Brown University in Providence, Rhode Island. He married my grandmother in Cincinnati and worked in sales for thirty-six years. He was a substitute teacher at Western Hills High School until 1994, a lector at St. Dominic Delhi Parish, a mentor at Oyler Elementary, and a volunteer at Cincinnati Children's, an activity he and my grandmother did together.

Grandpa loved *The Lawrence Welk Show*, the Cincinnati Reds, and the Bengals.

He was an Irish Catholic, short in stature. His hair was thick and dark, about the same texture as mine, didn't start graying around the temples until he was in his eighties.

My grandmother has lived a few miles from where she was born for her entire life. She's beaten cancer twice. I was too young to help the first time around, but when it returned in 2014, I flew back home and went off the radar for about a month to be with her.

My grandfather had passed away two years before, and I was terrified of losing her, too.

I spent a lot of time with my grandparents growing up. Anytime I was sick, I'd stay over there while my parents worked. My middle school was only a half mile from their home, so I'd often walk there after school. I watched bandleader and television host Lawrence Welk with my grandfather while he regaled me with tales from World War II.

It wasn't until later in life that I was more in tune with his dry and sarcastic sense of humor. When I was a kid, I took everything he said as gospel, so the factual war stories he told me intermingled with his fanciful and humorous exaggerations in my mind until they were the same. When he told me *he* killed Hitler, I believed him!

We'd often play war in the back room with little toy soldiers. He told the same tales over and over again, but I didn't mind. I liked hearing them all every time.

The stories he told me were usually broad and sweeping in scale, devoid of specific details. I would imagine he was happy to forget the particulars. The broad strokes were fascinating for a grandson to hear, but the gruesome realities were better left unspoken.

I'll never forget hearing my grandfather speak to the Junior Achievement program at Midway Elementary School about an Air Force buddy of his who didn't make it back. As tears welled up in his eyes, I felt so proud of him. (The school is gone now, but the sign remains; there's a shot of it in the opening credits of *The Andy Show* and the music video for "Ghost of Ohio," parts of which we filmed on what used to be the school grounds.)

I drew all sorts of pictures of KISS for my grandparents, which they displayed proudly. I believe my grandmother still has books full of them. Some are even matted and framed.

Urban and Anna went to mass every week. They were staunch John F. Kennedy Democrats. Jesus and politics were two of their favorite topics of conversation.

Both of them were highly educated. My grandmother worked as a chemist before she married and became a homemaker, raising my mom and four other children.

My grandmother and I share a taste for different foods nobody else in the family seems to like—things like black licorice candy, ginger snaps, those little orange gelatin wedges, and these tiny spice cookies from the Netherlands called Pfeffernüsse.

I spent so much of my time around the women in my family.

I sat with my mom, my aunts, and my grandmother (whom we call "Gran") and learned about the world through their perspectives. Although I've always loved hanging out with my cousins Joe, Alex, Henry, and Cyrus, I spent more time chatting with Heather and Melanie.

My grandfather was a traveling salesman, so my mother and her siblings were with my gran more often. My mom and her sisters created terrific lives and careers for themselves. My aunt Julie is a published author with a pair of paranormal thrillers and a handful of other books to her credit. (She's also a fan of the Reds and Bengals.)

The female perspective informed much of how I see the world. I had an easier time discussing politics or religion with women. So when I hear these stereotypes about them, I know them all to be stupid. Women don't know about politics? Female comedians aren't funny? Give me a break. I learned almost everything from women.

My grandfather passed away while I was on tour in 2012. We were opening a string of shows for Mötley Crüe and Slash when it happened. I'd just gotten a phone that would work in Europe, but the minutes were expensive, and it was difficult to use on the road.

I was on our double-decker bus after a show in Vienna, Austria, trying to find a movie to watch with one of the guys in our road crew. We landed on *A Few Good Men*, which we followed with another Tom Cruise movie, *The Last Samurai*. After that ended, we turned on *Crank: High Voltage*, the second in Jason Statham's action/black-comedy series.

I laid there mildly entertained by the movies. I looked over at my phone and saw that my mom was calling me. Those minutes were expensive, and it was about three a.m., so I figured I should go to bed anyway and call her back when we had Wi-Fi.

The next morning, we were on the outskirts of Interlaken in the Swiss town of Bern, where we were scheduled to play the Greenfield Festival. I sat numbly watching people hang-gliding overhead as my mother explained to me that my grandfather was gone. I later put together that the call the night before had been my last chance to speak to him.

Jonathan Syverson has been my friend and tour manager during nearly every major event in my adult life. (He was the best man at my wedding.) I sat with Jonathan and explained to him that I would have to return home immediately. "I know we are playing shows with Mötley Crüe and Slash, it's a dream come true for us, but I'm sorry. I must go."

We canceled the remaining shows in France, Germany, Switzerland, and at Graspop Festival in Belgium. I flew back to LA, then Cincinnati. I slept for a few hours and then went immediately to the funeral service.

At some point during all of that, I put together a eulogy for my grandfather. After I read it, the priest asked if I'd like to have it printed in the church newsletter. He said he thought it was beautiful. (I didn't have the heart to tell him I was asked to leave St. Dominic elementary a decade earlier.) I gave it to him. My grandmother still has the newsletter.

My grandfather's death wasn't a surprise in so much as we knew his body was breaking down, as will happen to any of us who are fortunate to live as long as he did.

People often compare the elderly to infants, but a baby doesn't have the mental faculties to consider that what they're doing could be inappropriate or embarrassing. But for a grown man, an Ivy League–educated World War II veteran at that, losing control of his body and bits of himself to dementia...it had to be so hard for him.

My grandmother called me on one such occasion when my grandfather was frustrated and confused after he'd had a bodily function-related accident in the house.

He was sad and embarrassed that his wife had to clean up after him. Given that he's from the Greatest Generation, and how close I am with my gran, I figured she'd cut me some slack if I made a bad joke at her expense. "Grandpa, don't worry. This is how a marriage should be. One partner poops around the house, and the other one has to clean it up."

He started laughing hysterically. "You know what? I suppose you're right, Andy!"

It turns out that was the last time I spoke with him. The very last thing I ever said to my grandfather? A poop joke. I'm honestly pleased that I could make him smile.

As I mentioned, "In the End"—the first single from the third Black Veil Brides album, *Wretched and Divine: The Story of the Wild Ones*—was inspired by my grandfather.

Later, I learned that my grandfather had once written words that were very similar to mine.

Cyrus Flanders, my great grandfather, passed away about two weeks after my second birthday. The eulogy my grandfather wrote for him in 1993 was strikingly similar to what became "In the End," though I'd never seen it until after I'd written the song.

I love to show my grandmother videos of Black Veil Brides fans singing "In the End" at shows and festivals all around the world. Whether it's Brazil, Eastern Europe, Australia, or back home in Cincinnati, my grandmother firmly believes my late grandfather is there with me in spirit as the audience sings the words with the band. She loves to watch these videos. It's like she's collecting souvenirs of all the places he's visited with me.

She got to see it firsthand during Warped Tour at Riverbend Music Center in Cincinnati. I invited her on stage, and she took it all in from her wheelchair. It was incredible.

When her cancer returned, I simply knew I had to go home and spend as much time with her as possible. Given her advanced age, the prognosis just did not seem good whatsoever. By the time I got to Cincinnati, she had already dropped to about seventy-five pounds.

Her hair was very thin, and she could barely get around. I set up a little bed in the backroom where my grandfather used to sit in his favorite chair; I slept about forty feet from her bedroom. Sometimes I'd curl up in the hallway to make sure I could get to her quickly should she wake up in the middle of the night and need help with something.

She was in terrible pain, and we did everything we could to make her more comfortable.

The sprouted grain loaves made by Ezekiel Bread, which she nicknamed "Bible bread," were one of the things we discovered she could hold down. Almond milk was something else her stomach could handle that would give her a decent amount of nutrients. We found different types of socks to ease her leg pain. My mom washed and cut her hair.

I spent every day with her. Aunts and uncles would go with us to her chemotherapy treatments. My cousins, who had moved from Cincinnati, came to town to help, too.

Over time she started to improve. She just decided she was going to beat it. She told me every day that she would win, drawing tremendous strength from her Catholic faith.

As critical as I am of organized religion, I often point out that the people who loved and shaped me, who influenced me with many progressive ideas, were highly intelligent and deeply faithful. The two are not mutually exclusive. It's disingenuous for even the most militant of atheists to pretend that when faced with something like that, they wouldn't be open to having help from some sort of "higher power" of some kind.

I am not a believer in an omnipotent God figure, but I understand why some choose that path. I don't proclaim that all of those ideas are crazy, I just think they aren't for me.

If I see someone drawing something of value from a belief system, I'm not one to encourage or discourage it. I understand why some declare themselves "faithless" and condemn those who believe in anything spiritual. Still, I find it hard to identify as an "atheist" myself because I have problems with what I see as a new religion of atheism.

As someone who doesn't believe in God, I've never thought, "I need to get together with some other people and talk about this." Whenever I hear different atheist celebrities talk about their cause, I wonder, why is there a "cause"? It's fundamental to my core understanding of reality that there probably isn't a God. It's just how I feel. But I don't need to mobilize with some movement based around that or recruit other people.

I'm an admirer and fan of magician and comedian Penn Jillette, one half of the famous duo Penn & Teller and author of books like *God, No!*. As he's pointed out, considering that proselytizing and conversion are fundamental aspects of organized religion, certainly if a friend truly believes I have a chance to go to heaven and enjoy everlasting life but doesn't talk to me about it, that person is a pretty terrible friend. Think about it: if this friend is right, my eternal soul is in jeopardy—and if I'm right, nothing changes.

I bring this up because there is an amount of Catholicism specifically and faith generally that was integral to my upbringing, and I'm perfectly fine with that. It's not so much that I drew inspiration from the teachings of the religion as I was inspired by people who did.

I continue to maintain my belief system, or lack of a belief system, without giving it too much thought throughout the day. Since I've stopped drinking, I've certainly gotten more in tune with the spiritual side of my life, but that's personal. That's for me.

I recognize that my ideology is a bit of a catch-22. I don't believe in supernatural gods, but I am convinced my silent thoughts ("prayers") can affect the outside world. Part of me certainly hopes that someone or something "hears" those supplications. The strictest of atheists would never accept or condone that as reality.

Formulating an idea of some sort of spirituality, rekindling my roots, or embracing the idea that maybe I do have greater importance in a cosmic way, these are all things that have helped in the latest chapters of my life. But it's nothing that informs the music that I write nor the way that I interact with my audience, at least not in any direct way.

I'm grateful to God, angels, the universe, the great "big empty" or whatever we choose to call it, that my grandmother had her faith to carry through the dark times.

As of this writing, her cancer has been in remission for roughly three years.

I would also like to acknowledge my awesome paternal grandparents, Margaret and Dennis. My middle name was chosen in tribute to my dad's father. While I didn't spend as much time with them growing up as I did with my mom's side of the family, they have always been loving and kind to me, and I love and treasure them both tremendously.

9

HARVEY & BONES

I WAS BACK IN the public school system for middle school, which I found to be even worse than a Catholic school. Blessedly, Misfits' *American Psycho* aided in my rescue.

The Columbine High School massacre, in which two students in suburban Colorado launched a vicious assault on their classmates that left fifteen people dead (including each of them), took place just a few months before *Famous Monsters* was released. The Columbine killers were described as loners who wore black and listened to Marilyn Manson. The latter of which proved to be false, but not before near irreparable damage to a subculture that has, in truth, helped so many feel safe and empowered.

In the immediate aftermath of Columbine, there was a ban on all-black clothing at my school. Wearing band merchandise would result in immediate punishment. They suspended me for wearing a Dropkick Murphys T-shirt, and that thing was *green*. The conventional "wisdom" was that dressing in anything out of the ordinary, by whatever vague standards, was a distraction from the learning process. That included my *socks*.

I wasn't on drugs, getting into fights, or even getting bad grades. I was wearing *socks with stripes on them*. Once the principal said to me, in a very patronizing way, "Hey, I know what it's like to be different, Andy. I used to eat SPAM right out of the can!" Yeah. He used to eat a brand of processed meat out of the can, so he, like, totally understood why I related to things like the Misfits and Grant Morrison's Batman instead of my peers.

As it had always been, it wasn't so much that I was "unlikable" as it was that I kept to myself. I wasn't a pariah getting chased out of town with pitchforks and torches. It's much less sexy than that. I wasn't so much persecuted as I was dismissed and ignored.

Girls didn't talk to me. I hung out with a few skater kids who nicknamed me "Chunk" (I'd gained some weight) and frankly weren't really my friends. But I wasn't sad. My attitude was always, "These people are dumb. They don't get it. I'm going to be what I'm going to be." I drew a lot of inspiration from something Gene Simmons said in one of my VHS tapes. It may have been *Exposed* or *X-Treme Close-Up* or *Kiss Konfidential*. I'm paraphrasing, but basically he said not to get down on people who don't like cool things (like KISS) because "you understand something they just don't know about yet."

My affection for the dark continued to blossom as well. I dove more deeply into an increasing number of bands, discovering the Damned, Lords of the New Church, Sisters of Mercy, Skinny Puppy, and more monsters with whom I could sing along.

Soon I would utilize the words from a Misfits song to help change my life.

My parents recognized how hard I struggled in traditional school. I wanted more. I had to move on to something else, somewhere else. I needed to be at a place called SCPA.

The School for Creative and Performing Arts in Cincinnati is a magnet arts institution that boasts an assortment of famous alumni, including Sarah Jessica Parker of *Sex and the City*, Rocky Carroll from *NCIS*, Carmen Electra, and three of the guys from nineties boy band 98 Degrees. (Nick Lachey was a producer on *Taking the Stage*, a reality television series filmed at SCPA that ran on MTV for two seasons in 2009 and 2010.)

SCPA is an incredible place. It's part of the Cincinnati Public Schools system, but people outside of specific geographical borders (like my family) had to pay to attend. My parents couldn't afford to send me. Thankfully my aunt Marianne (whom we call "Mimi"), one of my mom's two sisters, graciously offered to pay half of the tuition we needed for me to go.

I was elated, not the least because it was a chance to reinvent myself as precisely the person I wanted to project to the world. Plus, anybody wishing to attend SCPA had to earn it.

At my audition for the school, I sang the title song from the Rodgers and Hammerstein musical, *Oklahoma!*. I didn't have any acting monologues in mind when I auditioned for the drama department, so I instead did a dramatic reading of the lyrics of the Misfits' "Dig Up Her Bones," from the *American Psycho* album. They liked it! I was accepted.

With my mom's (reluctant) help, I dyed my hair black for the first time before I arrived at SCPA. Thanks to her work with Elizabeth Arden, I'd seen her doing makeup several times. She'd take me with her to beauty salons where she'd apply colorful eye shadow to the little old ladies who wanted to look nicer for church while I entertained them with my showmanship. As an admirer of KISS, the Misfits, and early Mötley Crüe, I was always interested in what was happening. I loved the creative possibilities makeup facilitated.

The night after we dyed my hair, my mom taught me how to put eyeliner and nail polish on properly. She didn't have the "wet n wild" brand most punks were using, so I had to settle for dark brown. It was still exciting and cool to enter into this stage of self-expression and outward identity. I'd gotten a little bit taller and started to lose some of the extra weight. By the time the summer was over, I thought I looked like Sid Vicious.

I didn't last long in the vocal music department, which was devastating to me, because I knew I wanted to be a singer in a band. But I was into punk rock music, where the ability to sing "beautifully" isn't a requirement. (In 2013, I visited SCPA and made sure to tell the instructor who ejected me from that department that I'm now a professional singer.)

I didn't grow up wanting to be Johnny Depp. I'd have rather been Matt Skiba. I wanted to be in a band. But I pursued acting next because it was a chance to perform.

A man named David Roth became an important mentor. No, I'm not talking about the singer for Van Halen. Mr. Roth was the drama teacher at SCPA. On my first day at my new school, he approached me in study hall and invited me to audition for a play.

One of the things I'd learned from watching interviews with Gene Simmons was to fake it till I make it. When Mr. Roth asked if I'd ever acted before, I said, "Sure!" Gene's strategy was to seize an opportunity when presented and figure out the details later.

Mr. Roth cast me as Elwood P. Dowd in *Harvey*, the role made famous by Jimmy Stewart. Despite my lack of experience, he gave me the part outright, without a single audition. He saw something in me, which was a substantial boost to my self-confidence. I rehearsed. I worked at it. I was now an actor, like my cousin Joe Flanders at his school.

Mr. Roth gave me a chance to be on stage. He taught me how to connect with an audience, from simple things like eye contact to more esoteric ideas. Later, I was cast as the lead in playwright Howard Richardson's Appalachian folktale, *Dark of the Moon*.

After years of isolation in other schools, SCPA was something of a utopian bubble for me. I wore whatever I wanted to wear. I was fortunate to make a handful of close friends there—people who meant the world to me, like Chance Kilgour and Mia Carruthers. I made several friends at SCPA, but those two in particular were my first real introduction into socialization and any sort of "popularity."

It wasn't like everyone suddenly adored me, but I had a handful of friends and more people who generally knew who I was. Other kids talked to me. I was no longer shunned. As someone with no experience with any level of social acceptance, it quickly went to my head. I came off like I thought very highly of myself. It was reactionary.

The first time I met Mia, for example, she politely introduced herself before an audition. I said, "I'm Andy, and I'm going to be the lead in this show, so that you know, because I'm the greatest actor in the world." Now, in my mind, it was facetious. Now that people were talking to me, I felt that I could be more over-the-top with what I said.

They say one should "work smarter, not harder," but I did the opposite when it came to befriending Chance. I just thought he was so cool and so funny. One afternoon I was invited to fill in with his after-school improv group even though I was a freshman and they were all seniors. I knew a girl I liked was in the audience, so I just way overdid it. I didn't follow their choreography or anything else set up to make the scene work.

I made enough people laugh that my performance was passable. But even more importantly, Chance offered to give me a lift home. I didn't possess the social skills to tell him I wanted to hang out, so I invented this elaborate scenario to spend more time together. I said my family had just moved and I wasn't sure where my new house was; I continually gave him wrong directions on purpose so we could drive around longer and keep talking. I didn't want it to end. Eventually we got pulled over. Yes, cops were there at the dawn of our friendship, thanks to an easily avoidable situation of my creation.

My mom once told me that cats work with rusty toolboxes when it comes to their emotions. As interactions with my peers were so limited, I worked with one too. It was hard for me to figure out what "friend" meant until later in life. Ultimately being in a band was a crash course in how to interdepend on other people. The friends I did have at SCPA knew I meant well, and I enjoyed their company quite a bit. You know housecats want to be around you, they're just standoffish sometimes.

Before I had the opportunity to unload in interviews, there were students at SCPA that I didn't treat very well. I took everything that had been put on me and threw it back.

I covered my insecurity with a renewed swagger. I refashioned myself to be as extreme as possible in this regard. I made grand pronouncements. It was a combination of humor and ego, which undoubtedly just made me look like a jackass to most people.

It eventually carried into the early days of the band. It's evident in every magazine cover story where I declared our new songs to be better than Led Zeppelin or whatever. I saw it as intentionally grandiose and tongue-in-cheek.

It stemmed from that initial idea back at SCPA that if people were listening, I could say crazy stuff. And if I said wild things, they'd be curious to hear what the next outrageous claim may be. I was mostly concerned with moving the needle. The era in which Black Veil Brides emerged was saturated with bands doing metalcore and screamo. If I could get attention with these boisterous remarks, more people might discover our message.

At that age, I wanted to cast myself as the leader of the disenfranchised. I built this façade of conviction and strength as a way to mask and placate my sensitivities, but eventually those feelings grew into something legitimate and pure. It took some time.

Unfortunately, this newfound socializing and acceptance paved the way for some bad habits. It wasn't long before I'd lost interest in most classes. A few of the teachers weren't impressed by me; the ones who were would offer me a safe harbor in their classrooms. My creative writing teacher, for example, would let me hang out with her. I'd hide away in her classroom for much of the day, scribbling down lyrics and cartoons.

A group of talent scouts came to SCPA (via their relationship with a Cincinnati agency that put kids in local commercials) from the Mike Beaty Model and Talent Expo in Dallas, which is essentially a weird "children on display" festival. I don't know how else to describe it. If the kids chosen to go to Dallas are deemed worthy enough once they are there, they next go to Hollywood for pilot season, when the TV networks cast their new shows. (One of the scouts was Angie Grant, whose daughter Allie was on Showtime's *Weeds*.)

My impression was that they were in Cincinnati in search of kids with the typical "all-American" type look. Mr. Roth encouraged me to audition for them anyway. So, armed with a monologue from *Harvey*, I did. The scouts liked me! They came to my house and told my parents they thought I should come to Dallas and, most likely, Los Angeles. "He's got some basic skills and an interesting look. He should give it a go."

As I wasn't exactly excelling academically by that point anyway, I thought it made sense. It felt like a smart step. My plan, my fixation, was still to start a band, but the acting could be a means to an end while on that path. I wanted to seize the opportunity.

My mom accumulated enough vacation days at work that we were able to embark on this adventure together for several weeks. We spoke to the school administration, and they approved my trip. (After all, a kid from SCPA getting cast in a pilot or commercial would only reflect well on them and encourage new enrollments.)

Our first stop was Dallas, Texas. Then we made our way to Hollywood.

10

OAKWOOD & METH

WE MOVED INTO A place in Toluca Hills called Oakwood, which bills itself as a "full-service housing community for children and their parents."

In other words, it was for kid actors and their stage parents.

Oakwood is a controlled access complex with 1,100 apartments situated close to all of the major film and television studios, as well as dance studios and acting workshops. They offer a Child Actor Program, which educates parents and kids about the business.

There was a documentary called *The Hollywood Complex* released in 2010, in which the filmmakers moved into Oakwood and chronicled the trials and tribulations of about a half dozen families whose kids were trying to "make it."

The listing for the movie on Amazon rightly describes it as both "hilarious and heartbreaking."

Oakwood was a place for aspiring child actors from all over America to come to during the pilot season and try to get cast in roles like "Cute Kid No. 5" on different shows.

Erik Per Sullivan, who played the youngest brother on *Malcolm in the Middle*, lived right next to me at Oakwood. Jeremy Sumpter from *Friday Night Lights* was there too.

Jennifer Lawrence was one of the kids who'd moved to LA and lived at Oakwood with her mom. She and I were born the same year. She grew up only one hundred miles or so from Cincinnati, in Louisville, Kentucky. About five years before her breakout role in *Winter's Bone*, mutual friends set me and Jennifer up on a blind date. We went to see *V for Vendetta* at the AMC Universal CityWalk 19. My mom drove us to the movies.

Jennifer wasn't interested in me.

I had plenty of meetings with agents and managers while we were in Los Angeles.

I auditioned for Tony Kaye, a six-time Grammy-nominated music video director, born in London to Orthodox Jewish parents, who worked with Johnny Cash, Roger Waters of Pink Floyd, and Red Hot Chili Peppers. He's known best as the director of the late nineties Edward Norton drama *American History X*, a troubled production that resulted in a spectacular career flameout for the filmmaker that became the stuff of Hollywood lore.

Kaye directed a series of public service announcements for the Montana Meth Project, a nonprofit group whose work was aimed primarily at teenagers. As a newly thin kid with black hair who could pass as an Edward Scissorhands cosplayer, it was pretty easy for me to get cast as a methamphetamine-addled weirdo. I relished the experience.

One of the highlights was meeting Edward French, an Oscar-nominated makeup artist whose credits included *Amityville II: The Possession* (1982), *Creepshow 2* (1987), and, most famously, *Terminator 2: Judgment Day* (1991). In more recent years, he's worked on *Terminator Salvation* (2009) and episodes of *2 Broke Girls* and HBO's *Westworld*.

I could've stayed in Ed's trailer doing makeup with him forever. Watching him work was like a crash course in the special makeup effects art form. I was fascinated.

A week or two after booking the Montana Meth Project PSA, I landed a commercial for AT&T. The house party themed ad, "Confetti," started airing in April 2006. I wore a white shirt and tie. (Yes, both of these projects can be found on YouTube.)

When we decided to move back home to Cincinnati, people were like, "That's crazy! There are actors here who starve for years before they can book a single thing!"

I was very cognizant of the value of the opportunities given to me, but we couldn't afford to stay in Los Angeles much longer. Since acting wasn't my first passion, I found myself getting more anxious to get started with music. The acting could wait. I enjoyed the craft of acting, but I wasn't chasing fame for its own sake, as a lot of kids (and their parents) were. The most important thing to me when I was fourteen was my dream to write songs that connected with people. I didn't want to end up a teen actor tabloid story, either. *TMZ*? I wanted to be in *Alternative Press*, *Kerrang!*, and *Revolver*. I wanted to be in *Rolling Stone*.

I met a kid named Vinnie at an improv class in Van Nuys right around the time I decided to move back. He and a friend of his started an early version of a YouTube channel called Breakfast Toms, which became pretty popular. (Eventually, they both abandoned acting and comedy for a career in EDM.) One day in class, he told me he had plans with a girl named Scout, an actress who'd made a movie called *Sleepover* with Steve Carell.

Vinnie was meeting her at Universal CityWalk, which is where we hung out all of the time since it was walking distance from Oakwood. I sort of invited myself to hang out with them.

Vinnie never showed up to meet her there. But I did.

I moved back to Cincinnati the day after we met, but we'd hit it off, so we stayed in touch via text (probably on our T-Mobile sidekicks or whatever we had back then).

Unbeknownst to me, my fate at SCPA was sealed just after I'd left Cincinnati.

I hoped to be celebrated upon my triumphant return home. What happened instead broke my heart. The administrators had promised I could continue my schoolwork remotely. They even handed me a massive binder full of materials before I left. But the director who brought the talent scouts to SCPA in the first place was no longer there.

His replacement didn't see the merit in my trip. When I got back, he told me that none of the work I'd done while

I was away would be credited. If I wanted to stay at SCPA, I'd have to agree to stay back a year. I was only a freshman. I couldn't imagine repeating a year of school. It's not like I'd been on some extended hiatus. I was gone for fewer than two months. I'd made some friends, gained a bit of popularity, and had a mentor in Mr. Roth, only to have the school admonish me for embarking on a trip they had encouraged.

They could have used the positive press from a student or two "making it" in Hollywood. As much as I loved that school and still cherish my time there, SCPA was rocked by several scandals, most of them involving sexual relationships between students and members of the faculty dating as far back as 1991. There were two more scandals of a similar nature in the early to mid-nineties. They didn't have much to brag about after Nick Lachey faded from the limelight. They did invite MTV to SCPA to make the reality show *Taking the Stage*, which featured my friend Mia as the lead, but it finished after just two seasons. (Despite only attending for fewer than two years, I appear on "notable alumni" lists.)

But the period from my adolescence I long for most remains the time when I was a student at SCPA. In quiet moments I'll allow my mind to wander back there. Not because I'm full of nostalgia about my past. It's more because I have so little nostalgia for other periods.

The school has since moved into a more modern complex, but when I'm in Cincinnati, I'll often visit the old building and sit on one of the benches in the empty field. (The old SCPA building also appears in the music video for "Ghost of Ohio.")

My year at SCPA was the only time I remember not being entirely fueled by this idea of revenge, this overwhelming obsession with "proving" myself to the outside world.

At SCPA I felt encouraged by people who understood me. I wasn't as driven by the idea that "I'll show them!" because there was no longer a "them" right in front of me daily. The people I'd viewed as adversaries were all somewhere else.

Having to leave SCPA brought back all those feelings of isolation.

11

SIXX & MYSPACE

No more teachers. No more classrooms. It was time to learn things via an internet modem.

The only requirement for homeschooling in Ohio at the time was to spend two hours per day using this software, which had no way of tracking how much work I actually completed. I was a voracious reader when it came to subjects that interested me, but nothing required for a traditional education was inspiring to me at all.

I wasn't lazy. I wanted to work. At fifteen, I took a three-dollar-per-hour job as a screen printer's apprentice at Art Works. We also did art installations for the city.

Every hour I wasn't at work, I spent on MySpace.

MySpace launched in the fall of 2003. It reigned as the largest social networking site in the world until its business model was copied and improved upon by Facebook (just as MySpace had copied and improved upon Friendster). At one point in the summer of 2006, MySpace was the most visited website on Earth. Yes, it was bigger than *Google*.

Not long after its celebrated $580 million acquisition by News Corp., MySpace became the butt of jokes. *Weekend Update* anchor Seth Meyers called it "the internet's abandoned amusement park" one night on *Saturday Night Live*. But at the time I discovered MySpace, it was a revelation. It was a place of community and belonging.

On MySpace, I found out there were a lot of other people around the world who were like me. It was a place where I could talk to people about European psychobilly bands like Demented Are Go and Mad Sin. I could make music myself and upload it to my profile.

"Friends" would put me in their "Top 8" because I looked interesting. At the time, I didn't know about From First to Last. I looked the way I did because of the Misfits and The Damned.

It was an underground scene where people responded to me. I recorded covers of songs like "Some Kind of Hate" and put them up for people who loved bands like Underoath to discover. It was frankly lovely to have these "friends" all over the world.

The first name people started to know me by was "Andy Sixx." It was never an intentional "stage name" for me. To tell you the truth, I had never thought about having a stage name. I never really thought about my last name. "Andy Sixx" was a product of MySpace, because regularly changing your name on MySpace was just a thing we all did. It was part of the whole MySpace "culture" that was happening at that time.

I don't think anybody saw himself or herself as a "brand" back then. I certainly did not. I had all kinds of different monikers. For the longest time, I went by Maniac Rocker from Hell, a reference to the song "Maniac Rockers from Hell" by UK psychobilly legends The Meteors, who have released over twenty albums since they formed in 1980. A girl I dated briefly in high school went by the name I Want a Black Jetta on MySpace, which was just a reference to a track called "Black Jettas" by the LA band Ima Robot.

Vanity Fair once called Christine Dolce "the Queen of MySpace," but it's hard to imagine she intended to be known as Forbidden in real life when she created her profile. (Sadly, Dolce passed away in 2017).

Most MySpace "celebrities" had random names that wouldn't work as stage names. Nobody is going to buy a record from "XXXXBradXXX" or "crushermonster_86." Notoriety was based more on whether or not someone's aesthetic matched what was becoming popular, if they took good photos, or if they had the right haircut.

I don't remember "vlogging" as a buzzword back then. Still, I figured it stood to reason that if people enjoyed looking at pictures of me dressed in a way that was very influenced by the horror punk of the Misfits and the theatrical vibe of KISS, then perhaps they'd like to see and hear what I had to say in videos, too. I had a particular perspective, a unique personality, and I felt like I had a sense of humor. So I started video blogging on MySpace.

I knew I wasn't blessed with the "stop traffic" type of looks to become famous for being good looking, nor did I have the resources to buy all of the cool clothes the scene kings wore. I didn't know cool aspiring photographers. My hair wasn't the "right" texture to do the same things as everyone else. But I was confident I could be authentic. I was sure I could build a following as long as my personality shined through in what I did.

I filmed everything with a little webcam (the cheap, round, external kind) and handled "post-production" in the painfully primitive (by today's standards) Windows Movie Maker.

Around the time I was making video blogs, I was shooting videos with Chance, my best friend from SCPA. We'd dress up in crazy costumes and act out skits mostly to entertain each other. Eventually, we uploaded them to a new website called YouTube.

The ridiculous selfies and flamboyant poses were just one element of my personality, as opposed to all of these guys on MySpace whose entire characters seemed to revolve solely around how handsome they were. (I'd imagine that whole subsection of the male model archetype has conventional haircuts today.) The end game for me was always to start a band. But I didn't see any groups at the time *nailing* what I wanted to do.

There was this German outfit, Tokio Hotel. One guy rocked the feminine eighties hair metal vibe, but it wasn't a uniform look for all of them. On the other end of the spectrum were bands with the hair metal look incongruously playing super aggressive metalcore.

Of course, there were throwback bands, but for them, it was mostly a big joke. Or at least that was my perception of groups like that at the time. Nobody was serving the exact interests that I had, which was some kind of combination of Billy Idol, Alkaline Trio, and KISS. I also wanted to incorporate the melody and spirit of punk rock and psychobilly music.

In my mind, Black Veil Brides would be a sort of heavy metal horror punk band.

I saw pictures of the LA band Glamour Punks and thought they came close to capturing the image I imagined. They were an influence on the early look of Black Veil Brides. But they weren't exactly taking the music world by storm.

I needed magazine covers. I wanted to be heard.

I set out to gain as much attention as I could via my MySpace video blogs. I figured that if I drew enough attention to myself, I could attract likeminded people to form my band with me and simultaneously establish a built-in following eager to hear the music.

I did everything I could to stay as active as possible: accepting friend requests, posting videos and photos, messaging, and commenting. I thought, "If I get enough people to notice me online, it doesn't matter whether there's anyone in Cincinnati who appreciates my vision or shares my passion for what I love. I will build something so impossible to ignore, somebody will have to pay attention to what I'm doing, and they will want to join."

In addition to the screen-printing job that filled my non-MySpace hours, I also worked at a modern art museum downtown, the Contemporary Arts Center, as part of a performance group that put on shows during school assemblies. My character was a mad scientist who taught kids how to be good students (and wore a terrible costume).

The woman who wrote the script was also the director (and my boss). Her stuff wasn't getting laughs. I wanted to connect with the crowd more like a stand-up comic.

They let me go from that role because I went "off book" and improvised my lines. The director screamed at me so loudly that kids stopped as they were leaving to watch what was happening as I stood there still wearing my stupid mad scientist outfit.

Then I had to ride with everyone back to where my car was parked downtown. It was when I was theoretically being "homeschooled," which was only accurate in the loosest of ways. (I suppose perhaps we could consider MySpace a form of "education.")

As I sat on the internet, I'd often have the George Reeves *Adventures of Superman* episodes from the fifties playing in the background. I pounded red Kool-Aid and devoured Original Premium Saltine Crackers two sleeves at a time. I'd get these Weight Watchers' chocolate ice cream bars, with the nuts on the outside, out of the freezer and stick about three spoonful's worth of Jif peanut butter on the outside of them. If I were still hungry, I'd put peanut butter and jelly on any remaining Saltines. That is what I would eat every day.

As the original "Andy Sixx" sat eating Saltines, my new girlfriend was in LA, advancing in her acting career. We were talking pretty regularly again around the time she filmed the *Halloween* remake, where she took on the lead role made famous by Jamie Lee Curtis.

As soon as the movie wrapped production, she came to Cincinnati to visit me. Like every girl I'd ever dated previously, I had lied to her about my age. I was almost two years younger than her but led her to believe we were the same age. (I never lied to my wife about my age; she just assumed I was older than I am, and eventually I just came out and confessed, "Hey, you know I'm only twenty, right?" She was surprised.)

I never wildly exaggerated my age. I kept it close to the age of the girl I was interested in but increased it enough to make it feel more "appropriate" for them. I dated a senior when I was a freshman, and she willfully believed I was the same age as her, even though she knew we weren't in the same grade. Maybe she figured I was held back several times.

After my girlfriend's visit, I was more determined than ever to get to California and start my career in earnest. I knew I had to double my commitment to the plans I'd always had, the same dreams I formulated and wanted to execute way back in elementary school.

I wanted to get in shape. I needed to look cool. I had to form this band I had in my head.

I knew spending all day online wouldn't be enough to pass the time, so I decided to make another attempt at school. Given that I hadn't stepped foot in one in a year, I was in full-on fairy-tale land. I dressed like Malcolm McDowell as Alex in Stanley Kubrick's adaptation of *A Clockwork Orange*, with a long mullet in the back and a Misfits style "devilock" in front.

While homeschooled, I grew accustomed to wearing these fanciful costumes and teasing my hair up like RATT's Stephen Pearcy in the "Round and Round" video. I'd forgotten that these kids didn't like me in elementary school, and I was far less crazy looking then. So now I show up to high school with red eye shadow, tight white shirts, skintight jeans, the whole deal, and "surprisingly," kids were not responsive to that look.

Also, there weren't any records of the work I'd done at home. It was such an early form of software there was no way to transfer that over to the official records. It was the Wild West in those days. Nobody was monitoring me. There was no truancy officer at the door. And truthfully, I was never actually doing it. I'd shut the laptop and go on MySpace.

As a result, they placed me in seventh-grade level English class and special education level mathematics. I enjoyed government class because it presented an opportunity to debate. But this was the Midwest during the George W. Bush administration, so it wasn't long before the government classroom showed me the door.

On the plus side, Dave Navarro was on television, so a few girls started to pay attention to me. But dudes

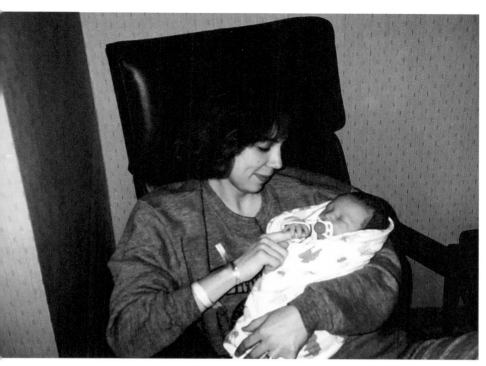

First picture with Mom

With Dad circa 1991

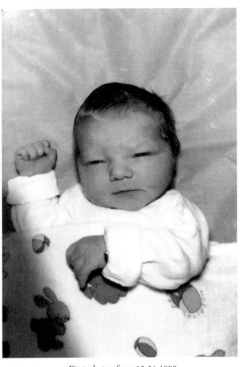

First photo of me 12-26-1990

Mom and Dad at my baptism

Dad doing the famous "flying Andy"

My first Halloween

Early photo with my dad

The coolest outfit anyone has ever worn

Circa 1994

Grandma and Grandpa Biersack

Gran and Grandpa Flanders' wedding

My first dog, Cooper. He was my best friend at that age.

Playing catch with Grandpa Flanders

Doing my best Barry Larkin impression

*Dad and I getting ready for a Bengals game
at Riverfront Stadium*

Family trip to Martha's Vineyard, age seven

Heading to a Bengals game with my cousin Alex in the early '90s

The goat

Me and Mom 1998

With Grandpa Biersack

Batman Forever *VHS 1995*

Hockey drawing, age nine

WWF and Batman drawings, age nine

FrankenAndy and counsins Cy and Alice

Hanging with Batman beyond

It stings! Halloween

Winning goalie skills awards in Detroit at the North American Roller Hockey Championship

Playing hockey for the Cincinnati Storm

Playground hockey in St. Louis visitng my grandparents

Whodey

Playing hockey at Golden Skates in Cincinnati

My first time playing hockey in our basement

Me with Grandpa Flanders at the hockey dome in Mason, Ohio

Hanging with Grandma and Grandpa Biersack

Winning football camp "offensive lineman" award

St. Dominic's little league baseball card

Playing little league baseball

Me and Joe on Easter with the family

Me and Joe after a play he was in circa 2001

Basement hockey in 1996

Dressed as Gene Simmons in the living room, 1997

The cover of my "biography" I wrote and illustrated at age ten

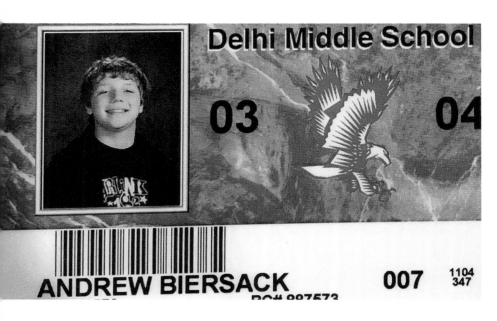

Delhi Middle School

03

04

ANDREW BIERSACK

007

1104
347

My Delhi Middle School ID, 2003

St. Dominic Catholic School photo

The outside of the old SCPA building in 2006

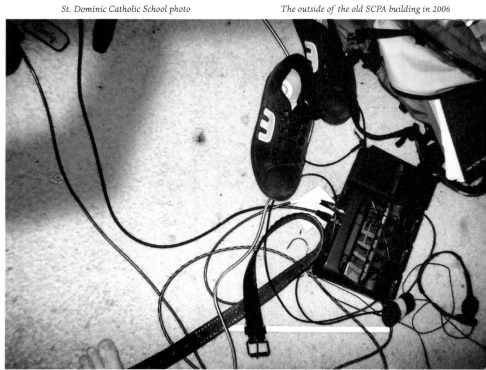

Bedroom 2004

Rockin' my makeshift "drum set"

Christmas 2004

My old toy set ups:
Misfits toy stage, batman figurines,
two of my many KISS toy stages

My typical high school outfit

Me at age fourteen at St. Joseph cemetary. We later filmed parts of "The Ghosts of Ohio" video here

Me and Gran circa 2005

My typical high school outfit

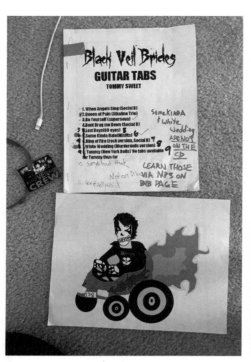

Book I would give to people to audition to early BVB, featuring handmade "crew" lam and "Biersack artwork"

Favorite T.U.K. creepers in high school

Early handmade stage props

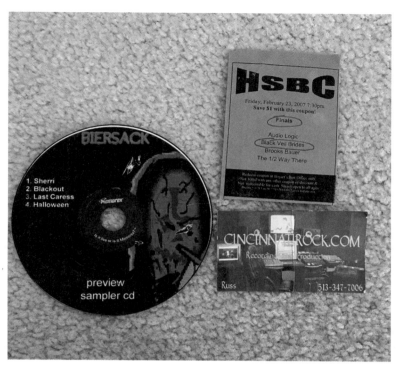

Early "Biersack" demo and battle of the bands flyer

Freshman year at SCPA

Filming "Jumped" Montana Meth ad

My original BVB logo design sketch, 2006

After my first performance in "Harvey" at SCPA with Grandpa and Aunt Julie

Garage "Biersack" rehearsal

Early BVB gig at the Mad Hatter in Covington, KY

Black Veil Brides on stage in 2008

*Singing all my songs to my
bedroom mirrors*

First "Biersack" show at an art gallery in North Cincinnati, 2007

Performing at the Mad Hatter with Chris Stewart in 2008

Me and Patrick Fogarty during the filming of "Knives and Pens"

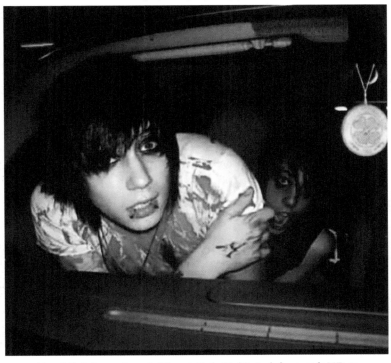

Me and Chris Stewart in my Cadillac outside the Mad Hatter before an early BVB gig

BVB merch money from an early show

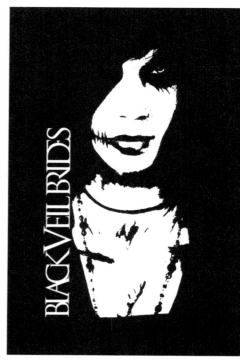

First BVB Hot Topic shirt

Halloween show in 2010

Broken nose in a hotel in London, 2012

BVB tour bus, 2014

Cincinnati

When we crashed the VMAs red carpet (uninvited)

Set the World on Fire 2011

Backstage at Warped Tour in 2011

At the scene of the crime with my dad, standing in the location of the ribs incident a year later

Jeremy Danger

Scott Uchida

Black Veil Brides wretched and divine era

Black Veil Brides Alive and Burning filming

Sitting with Gran at the 2015 Vans Warped Tour

My concept design for "The Mourrner" 2012 stage costume

My concept design for "The Mystic" 2012 stage costume

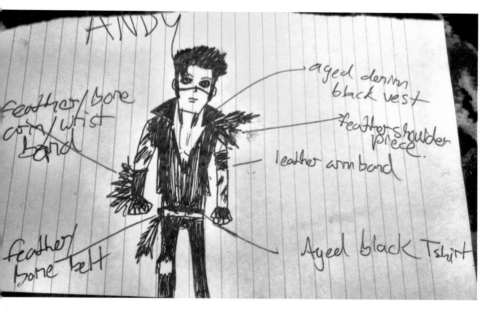

My concept design for "The Prophet" 2012 stage costume

My concept design for "The Destroyer" 2012 stage costume

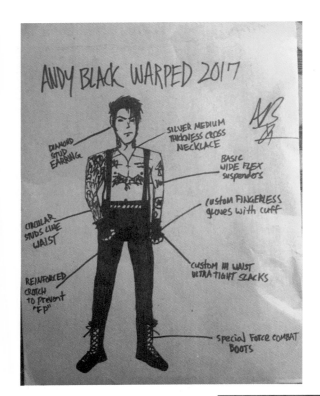

My design for the 2017 Andy Black stage outfit

My first "Ghosts of Ohio" concept painting

My storyboard for the "Westwood Road" music video

My storyboard for the "Ssants of the Blood" video

Sitting with Bob Rock during the recording of BVB 4

During the infamous Golden Gods speech

Scott Uchida

Backstage before the taping of "Alive and Burning," 2014

Me and Bob Rock during vocal tracking week for BVB 4

Marrying the love of my life

Our wedding day 4-16-16

Lizzy Cupcake

Jinxx and CC with Gran at our wedding

Me and Juliet with John and Amy Feldmann at our wedding

Backstage with Aunt Mimi, Gran, Aunt Julie, and Mom

Mom, Juliet, and me with a new friend

Me and Gran circa 2019

Me and Juliet backstage at BVB Roxy residency

With David Roth (SCPA), 2019

Hanging with Ryan J Downey

With Mom and the batmobile

With Jake tracking "The Night"

In the studio with Feldy during the making of "The Ghosts of Ohio"

In the studio writing
"The Ghosts of Ohio"

Me, Ryan, and Joe

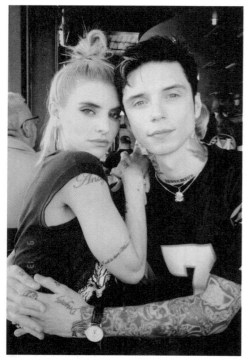

The love of my life

With Blasko at a 2016 Universal Records party

Family, summer 2019

Black Veil Brides live in Mexico, 2020

Aaron Berkshire

were straight-up throwing rotten fish in my locker like exaggerated bullies in an eighties teen movie. I had to learn to defend myself in physical confrontations. I never became much of a fighter, but fights would find me.

These skirmishes led to the administration sticking me in a trailer a mile and a half away from school with, like, seven old computers and one teacher. It was the place where the school system hid away the riffraff they couldn't necessarily expel but were tired of suspending over and over again.

In a fantastical cinematic version of this story, the discarded miscreants would accept me as one of their own and ultimately decide to make me their king. But that's not what happened. The people in that trailer thought even less of me than the "normal" kids.

All of the schoolwork in that trailer felt like a waste of time. The staff had us watch Will Smith's *I Am Legend* and write essays about the apocalypse. One school "assignment" in that trailer involved analyzing the nuanced differences between the patriotic anthems of Toby Keith and the patriotic anthems of Alan Jackson. So I started skipping school.

I'd leave the house in the mornings and drive my 1996 Geo Metro to a Dunkin' Donuts parking lot where I'd sit in my car smoking cigarettes all day till school was over.

Sometimes I'd drive to the cemetery and just sit there, vividly imagining funerals. I was never disrespectful. I was more sort of reverent, in awe of the pageantry of these giant statues and mausoleums dedicated to the departed.

I would visit LA as often as possible. There was a short-lived low-cost airline, Skybus, which flew from Columbus to LA every day for just $95.95. It was like Southwest Airlines stripped of all the chairs. They were terrible planes, and there was no food service.

I'd drive to Columbus or Cleveland, wherever I'd found the best flights, and land at LAX, Bob Hope Airport in Burbank, and even John Wayne Airport in Orange County.

I was determined to build a life for myself in Los Angeles and to move there when I turned eighteen. I had about six thousand dollars from my commercial work coming to me on my eighteenth birthday. (In my mind, at the time, that was probably enough to buy a house.)

Everybody who was ever in any iteration of Black Veil Brides, from 2006 till 2008, heard my constant promise that I'd head for Hollywood when I turned eighteen. I said they were welcome to join me, but I was doing the band with or without them. Moving was *always* my plan.

During one of my visits to Los Angeles, I walked into an F.Y.E. store and saw CDs from I Am Ghost and Escape the Fate on the endcaps. It made me so angry. I wasn't mad at those bands, I was pissed off that my (imaginary) album wasn't on display next to those CDs. I felt like I was wasting time every second that I wasn't living in Hollywood.

It had to be a tumultuous experience for my parents. But like always, they backed me up and worked as hard as they could to make my dreams happen.

It was more important than ever to me that I looked the part. I willed myself to become what I had envisioned. It was part artifice, part bravado, and all determination.

There were a lot of bondage shops and artists around in this avant-garde neighborhood in Cincinnati's Northside. There used to be a place called Scentiments Rock City, which is now out of business, where I got a lot of my clothes. They'd let me order out of a Lip Service catalog. They also had GG Allin and Elvis Costello shirts, which may have been bootlegged by them; they were just cheap white shirts with very simple images.

I ordered these green leopard print T.U.K. Creepers out of the Lip Service catalog at Scentiments after I saw Geoff Kresge, the stand-up bassist for Tiger Army, wearing them at Vans Warped Tour. The day they were delivered to the store was a big deal to me. My mom drove me down there to pick them up, and I wore those things to school every day.

Warped Tour was such an essential part of my journey, first and foremost, as a fan.

12

WARPED & WARMTH

I WENT TO MY first Vans Warped Tour in 2001. I remember thinking it was the best day ever ("Best Day Ever" was the slogan for one Warped, years later). I saw Dropkick Murphys, AFI, Rancid, Groovie Ghoulies, and the Phenomenauts, all at that first show.

I went to Warped every year till I moved to LA. I caught Avenged Sevenfold as they were first getting massive. I got to see The Living End from Australia. Around the time bands like Underoath and From First to Last were getting popular on Warped Tour, the way I looked, my hair and my clothes started to feel a little bit more "accepted" there.

I often went to shows sporting thick eye makeup, a tiny T-shirt, like seventeen belts or whatever around my waist, and those T.U.K. Creepers on my feet. I was wearing some variation of this uniform when I went to see one of my favorite bands at the time, Street Dogs, a punk group from Boston formed by the original vocalist for Dropkick Murphys.

They were doing a signing, and I was incredibly psyched. I was looking forward to meeting Mike McColgan, who sang on Dropkick's classic debut album *Do or Die*.

As a young kid with a voice as deep as mine, people assumed there was something wrong, like maybe I was sick or dying. My throat was likely extra hoarse at the Street Dogs concert from cheering and singing along. I met the singer and told him I loved *Do or Die* and how much I wanted to grow up to be like him.

He kind of motioned for me to get away from him. "You sound like you're sick right now." He said to the people around him something to the effect of, "I can't have this kid coming over here and making me sick." I felt like a deflated balloon. "*Are* you sick?" he asked.

By that point, I felt so hurt by the question I just simply said, "Yes."

"What do you have?"

I shook my head. "Oh, no, nothing you can catch," I said. "It's not like *that*."

My teenaged upset far outweighed the reservations I should have had about allowing someone to believe I was terminally ill, which was the clear implication, even if I didn't come right out and say it definitively. I let him think that because he'd been "mean."

I don't tell this story to make him look bad to fans of Street Dogs. He probably had a particularly bad day. Hell, I may have misremembered some detail of it.

It would have been nice if he were a little bit less dismissive. While I certainly understand why any singer is hyper averse to catching a cold or worse while on tour, this was a pivotal moment for me. I thought, "If I ever have the opportunity to be in a situation where someone is excited just to meet me, I will remember how important that moment is to a fan. I have to be careful always to be as considerate as I can manage." I haven't always lived up to the promise I made to myself about meeting fans, but I do always try.

I learned another valuable lesson, too. On that day, I discovered that not everybody making these CDs I listened to was going to be my friend. Later in life, I understood that his dismissiveness wasn't anything personal. It didn't mean he didn't want to connect with a fan. Particularly for a vocalist, it's essential to stay healthy on the road. He may have been right to back away from the "sick" kid in his face. I was probably overly sensitive.

The connection Black Veil Brides has with our fans has meant everything. I could fill this entire book trying to list all of the incredible stuff fans have done for us and given to us. I'm sure that Mike McColgan feels the same way, regardless of that particular day.

Years later, I recounted this story in an interview, and Street Dogs caught wind of it. Much to his credit, Mike went out of his way to invite me onto their RV one summer on the Warped Tour. He handed me a drink, apologized, and regaled me with old road stories.

I was very appreciative that he went out of his way to do that.

Luckily, I'd already met one of my heroes before that experience, and it was everything I could have wanted it to be. Eric Singer from KISS was the first person of any stature in music to give me positive encouragement about being onstage. When I was seven or eight years old, my dad took me to the Indianapolis KISS Expo, a long-running fan convention that's thrived no matter what the state of KISS was at any given time in the mainstream. (Singer and ex-guitarist Bruce Kulick performed at the 1998 convention.)

Remember, Eric Singer was the drummer on *Revenge*, the first KISS album I ever bought. He's the guy playing drums in the video for "Unholy." He was born in Cleveland, Ohio, and grew up a KISS fan himself. Years later, he was wearing the Catman makeup and playing all of the KISS hits on world tours through 2020.

As a kid, I went to a few baseball card conventions, where we met different athletes and got autographs. One of the more exciting things for me was meeting Javier Lopez, a catcher for the Atlanta Braves, in East Cincinnati. It was the Sports Card Memorabilia & Autograph Show, held annually at Archbishop Moeller High School in Hamilton County, which started in the early eighties. A lot of the athletes who came weren't famous yet. Javier Lopez went on to win the World Series with the Braves in 1995.

Before the KISS Expo, that card show was my only experience around celebrities or famous people. So even meeting a KISS *tribute band* was a big deal. I got an autograph from the guy who played drums as the Catman in the group Mr. Speed. It was overwhelmingly cool to be surrounded by so many KISS fans and merchandise. It was a pocket of the universe where the things I loved were celebrated, not shunned.

Anything there was to do at KISS Expo I wanted to do. They had a karaoke competition in the middle of the hall, and Eric Singer was the judge. It was during the period where he was out of KISS before he returned in the Catman makeup after the reunion era line-up disintegrated. I sang "Deuce," from the band's self-titled debut album.

I did all of the moves. I had been practicing for this moment my entire young life, so I didn't have stage fright. I've been insisting since the time I could talk that people should watch me do things, so there were no "nerves." And people were excited about it!

Here was this precocious kid doing all of the Gene Simmons stuff, whipping out my tongue, emulating his voice, and everything that came with it. If I went back and did this at a KISS Expo as an adult, nobody would think it was cool. But a little kid can get away with a lot more.

When people asked Eric Singer what he thought about my performance, he said all of these nice things about me. I don't recall what he said explicitly; I was still very young, after all. I just remember the sentiment and that his vibe was warm and positive. That was my first interaction with anyone who was a musical "star" to me; the fact that he was so supportive meant the world. Sure, he was an adult being kind to a little kid, but I took it very seriously.

Fast-forward to 2015. I was standing on the side of the stage watching Ozzy Osbourne at the Monsters of Rock Festival in Sao Paulo, Brazil, where Black Veil Brides had performed on the same bill as Ozzy, Judas Priest, Motörhead, and yes, KISS.

I stood next to Eric Singer as he told me how much he liked Black Veil Brides. Both he and Tommy Thayer (who took over for Ace as the Spaceman in KISS in 2002) approached us and invited us to be their guests at Download Festival, which was coming up soon. I did not mention our previous encounter at the KISS Expo.

I knew what I wanted to do with my life way back then before I'd even met Eric Singer. The encounter with the singer of one of the bands I loved on Warped Tour sharpened my edges. It gave me renewed focus and drive about what I wanted to do and exactly how I wanted to go about it. Black Veil Brides was like a movie I'd scripted in my head.

It was time to go about casting that film and getting it greenlit by Hollywood.

13

PUNKS & PAINT

I now had real stage experience thanks to Mr. Roth at SCPA. Agents and managers in LA taught me how to find people and talk to them. So, it was time to form my band.

When I went to auditions in Los Angeles, they'd give you a script. I decided to take this approach to assemble my players. I put together a book full of tablature of tracks by Social Distortion, the New York Dolls, Alkaline Trio, the Misfits—a bunch of songs I wanted people to learn so we could cover them. I included several visual references as well—pictures of Samhain and *A Clockwork Orange*. I was a teenager handing a book to people in their twenties and confidently saying, "Study this if you want to join my band."

Before "Black Veil Brides," the moniker I chose was merely eponymous. I took a page from Danzig and Billy Idol with "Biersack." But I started to crave a three-word name, something that would sound killer when people chanted it. I liked the positive and negative juxtaposition of "Guns N' Roses" and "Velvet Revolver." The worst part of any story is usually a funeral while one of the best parts, in movies and life, is a wedding.

"Black Veil Brides" hit that positive/negative juxtaposition I wanted. It was the culmination of my experiences as a snotty Catholic school kid enamored by the beautiful iconography yet equally sickened by the hypocrisy and brutality of the church.

Considering how active my father would eventually become on social media, it's funny to look back and remember how much hell he gave me about sitting at the computer all day using MySpace. He didn't get it. He'd be watching sports while I was on the computer and he'd ask me, "Hey, why don't you go outside and meet some people?" In his mind, the way to find band members was to go hang out at music stores and Guitar Center.

That was the way it used to be done, and I did take some of his suggestions about old school methodology. We put ads in *Cincinnati CityBeat*, our local alternative newsweekly, every single issue. Nobody responded. I scoured the other ads, too, and I never saw a single ad that referenced the bands I liked or the aesthetics I wanted.

These days, followers and "impressions" carry a particular currency in the business world. Nobody was talking about that back then. But I figured if I could get enough "friends" on MySpace, someone would join my band just to have access to that exposure.

I was right. Eventually, I was able to find people, even at the music store. I met a guy who was playing "God Called in Sick Today" by AFI on guitar. I thought to myself, "Okay, that works. I know that song." I had social anxiety in most situations, but when it came to the steady process of following my "blueprint" for my ultimate ambition, those barriers fell. I struck up a conversation with this guy about AFI with ease.

Other times I'd find somebody who didn't like any of the things I loved but who was excellent at their instrument. It was a part of why I cycled through so many band members.

I know there are plenty of lead singers who exercise strict control over a group, but I wasn't some tyrant. I was a child! But people couldn't commit for any length of time, if at all. Some of them just weren't into the kind of bands that had inspired me. Understandably, a guy weaned on country music from a farm in Northern Kentucky, who will do anything to be in a band, is only going to stomach me painting half of his face like a skeleton and putting him in a studded vest to play the Lexington State Fair for so long.

Outside of playing hockey, the band dynamic was my first real group social experience. I didn't have much in common with these older guys from Northern Kentucky whom I'd convinced to take a chance with me, but the drive to play music overruled most everything else. I craved that "gang" mentality I'd read about with classic bands. I hadn't cared much for fitting in before, but I wanted my bandmates to like me.

There was a revolving cast of local and semi-local characters who came and went.

Lead guitarist Chris Stewart was a kid from Covington, Kentucky, with a pretty cool MySpace name for that era, "Christopher Curbstomp." He was in the band for about a year, beginning in 2007. We wrote "Knives and Pens" together during that time.

At one point, Black Veil Brides had a forty-five-year-old drummer, Frank. He knew my dad and wanted to do his kid a favor. He found it all entertaining and was down to help me out. I have nothing but complimentary things to say about him. If I were in his shoes, I don't know that I would have done it. But that's because I'm not as good of a guy as Frank.

Our first show was at an art gallery in that Northern Cincinnati neighborhood, where I bought those Creepers at Scentiments Rock City. We had to wait till like two a.m. to play. We did Billy Idol and Alkaline Trio covers. Poorly. (I don't recall the entire setlist.)

Black Veil Brides was less of a band at this point and still more of an "idea." The songs weren't so much "good" as they were "good enough," considering my age and experience.

I wanted to capture that same feeling I had when I went to see Dropkick Murphys and AFI, the attitude that maybe I didn't have to be so lonely. The outside world didn't seem so indifferent when I was in these rooms with these people. The band on stage didn't have to know I was there for what they were saying to speak to me. It was a genuine connection.

These are sentiments any disenfranchised kid desperately wants to experience. Dropkick didn't even have to sing about misery and pain. It was impossible to feel sad while singing along to a catchy Dropkick gang vocal chorus about unity and empowerment. Whatever that special "thing" was about bands like Alkaline Trio, it became my thing. It was *mine*.

My hair was huge. I would spray it with Aqua Net Super Hold spray and while it was still wet take a flat iron and fry it. My whole head was covered in liberty spikes that were these thin fans created in a way that just destroyed my hair. I did that every day, so I had these spikes and points and then these giant bangs. I wore button-up shirts, bowties, and white batting gloves made for baseball.

As the band was getting going and I was using the MySpace profile to promote what we were doing, the name Andy Sixx just sort of stuck. At some point, there was a "Biersack" Myspace page, which eventually became the Black Veil Brides MySpace page. After that first show, we played basements, garages, and a high school battle of the bands.

Any version of the band would set up in the garage or kitchen, usually. My parents let me take the table out of the kitchen, which was very cool of them. I would use a little handheld video camera to record us and then post it on MySpace. We also had a Sony digital multitrack recorder. We recorded cover songs primarily. One of the guitar players had a sister named Sherri, so we renamed our version of Alkaline Trio's "Sadie" to "Sherri."

The first thing I "released" in my life was under the name Biersack. It was three songs: "Wait for the Blackout" by The Damned, "Hybrid Moments" by The Misfits, and "Sherri." I didn't know how to play bass, so I just made up bass lines; it's just absolute lunacy. I'm just playing whatever, and it came out loud and clear through my little amp.

I did the artwork on a PC in Microsoft Paint. We bought CD labels at Best Buy and printed every single one of them out. I smeared the ink, trying to put the labels on the CDs. I told everyone at school that this was going to be the biggest band ever, passing out CDs.

My first experience in a real recording studio was in the City of Forest Park, a northern suburb of Cincinnati, for what became the *Sex & Hollywood* EP. Forest Park was home to The Forest Fair Village shopping mall. I mean, technically it's still there, but once abandoned, it was basically reclaimed by nature. They just let it go. I was looking at pictures online, and there are, like, trees growing in the food court. It looks creepy.

Speaking of creepy, Forest Fair Village is also where I saw *The Adventures of Pinocchio*, an unintentionally disturbing live-action movie directed by Steve Barron, who made some of the most influential music videos of the eighties: "Take On Me"; "Money for Nothing"; "Africa" by Toto; "Antmusic"; "Billie Jean." *The Adventures of Pinocchio* (twenty-seven percent on Rotten Tomatoes) was the subject of a 2020 episode of the *How Did This Get Made?* podcast, a few months before the Alamo Drafthouse screened it for "Weird Wednesday," describing it as "the most horrifying kids movie of 1996." That field trip was where I discovered my love of Junior Mints candy, so it was a banner day for me all around.

The recording studio was near The Underground, a Christian rock venue that at one point or another booked all sorts of bands: Switchfoot, Demon Hunter, Red, Jars of Clay, even twenty one pilots when they were on the way up. Of course, they never invited Black Veil Brides to perform there—not because we had done anything explicitly "anti-Christian," it was just a safe assumption that we weren't the right kind of band for them.

One of the other guys found the studio. We had pooled enough money together to be able to record two or three songs. In retrospect, everything about the studio is what we might today call "extra." The gentleman who owned the place treated the whole proceedings like we were entering Sound City or Abbey Road or something. Way too fancy of a lobby area. Way too many snacks. It seemed like this guy's goal was to be king of a recording studio, and we were participating in his dream with him.

Pro Tools was new to me, as were all of the noises available to us. I was very enamored by all of the different sounds that you could make in a professional recording studio. "Well, can we make it sound like a helicopter? Or an explosion?" That's how all of those things ended up in the songs.

It wasn't a new experience for me to hear my voice. After all, I would make everyone film me doing the entire

Phantom of the Opera or *Sweeney Todd*, or KISS's *Greatest Hits*, singing in the living room at five years old and badgering everyone to watch me.

I didn't write much of any of the songs that we recorded that day— "A Devil for Me," "Hello My Hate," and "Sex & Hollywood." The lyrics don't read at all like anything I later wrote myself. At the time, I wrote primarily about horror punk things, like zombie girlfriends. I was fifteen. I didn't have any real experience as a songwriter. The other guys in that iteration of the band were older, like eighteen or nineteen. They were able to talk about things that I hadn't experienced. Plus, they drank, they smoked cigarettes, all of that stuff.

I'm not trying to be mean, but "Sex & Hollywood" is basically what an eighteen-year-old in Northern Kentucky might *imagine* "Hollywood" to be like, based on movies and TV. Hey, there was a Murderdolls song called "Dead in Hollywood," so that was similar enough for me to be excited by it. But I didn't have any personal affinity or connection to those songs.

I just thought, "Well, I super want to have a band, and these songs are cool enough." To this day, people ask why those songs haven't made it onto an official release. I certainly don't want to disparage anyone who may like them. I just have no connection to them.

I tend to forget this, but I did write the chorus and some other bits in "A Devil for Me" and parts of the verses of "Sex & Hollywood." I wrote absolutely nothing on "Hello My Hate." So, I was involved, but nothing like I would eventually be. By the time we made "We Stitch These

Wounds" and "Mortician's Daughter," I came up with the concepts and lyrics.

We used CD Baby to get those first three songs onto iTunes, made a few CDs, and we put them on MySpace. That was about it. I was not a fan of any of the songs, but it was the only material that we had. And they didn't sound very good. But I figured, "Well, this is it. If I'm going to get to the next rung, which is making more songs, I have to start with these songs first."

I didn't have a lot of buddies in real life; my "friends" existed in profiles on the internet. There weren't many people from the "hipper" social circles of the local scene who would give me the time of day. The person who was nicest to me sang in a band called Dichotomy. He wore a sock on his dick and nipple tape and behaved like a complete crazy person on stage. He would beat the crap out of himself and say things to the crowd like, "You are my goats!" The drummer was a bigger guy who took off his shirt and covered himself in King Diamond style face paint. Naturally, I loved those guys.

Nobody else was interested in playing with a teenager doing a wannabe Misfits meets KISS thing. The "cool" locals had skinny jeans, soccer shirts, and swoopy haircuts. The Cincinnati scene had plenty of "spirit-filled" Christian hardcore bands and militant straight-edge crews, neither of which I related to whatsoever. I wanted to create my own thing.

We had some supporters early on, but the more we stood out, the more scorn we invited. At one early show somebody even vandalized my parents' car in the parking lot.

There was a website with a message board called Cincy Punk, which at some point became primarily a place for the local scenesters to make fun of me. They seemed to take endless pleasure in bashing this little kid who was trying to be in a band.

They'd make crude Photoshop pictures of me. Once they took a photo of me performing and changed the microphone into a huge dick and balls going into my mouth.

The chance to prove them all wrong just further fueled my fire.

One thing that's funny about the whole polarization around Black Veil Brides is that it played perfectly into my innate drive, my contrarian impulse, to fight. Did I make all of these obstacles for myself simply so I could fight them? How often in our lives do we erect these massive walls simply to give ourselves something to leap over and achieve?

Our generation didn't seem to get as many opportunities to develop the proper skills for adulthood before thrust into an environment where we communicated with adults daily. We get so many examples of people who triumphed over some sort of adversity. Could this inspire some people to create that adversity?

Whether it was bravery, stubbornness, stupidity, or some combination of all three, I started taking a firm outspoken stance from the stage against different people in town while way too young to understand the potentially severe consequences of my actions.

I challenged local crews of bare-knuckled fighters well known for defending their beliefs with violence when they felt it necessary. I didn't use drugs or drink, either, but I saw most of these guys as bullies who weren't welcoming to outsiders like me.

I realize some seem to feel good about things that were just handed to them, but that has never been me. I have to know I fought for something tooth and nail for the victory to mean what it should to me.

I always endeavored toward increasing theatricality with every Black Veil Brides show. We bought skeletons from the Halloween store and covered them in blood onstage. My father happily footed the bill for all the old stage props and used clothing we could muster.

We gave out shirts to the audience for free, which was a trick I'd learned from KISS. They would paper the crowd with them, so record executives would see an audience full of KISS tees when they came to check out the band. I was getting the blank shirts from a surplus store, which resulted in Black Veil Brides designs out there printed on bright pink, neon green, mauve, burgundy, dirty browns, and every other color of cloth. I learned the same thing KISS and every sports team knew: people love free shirts.

I was fascinated by the Samhain *Initium* album cover, which featured the band shirtless and covered in blood. I wanted to figure out how they'd pulled it off. I was a teenager, and Samhain was long gone, so I never got to see them do their "blood show" live.

For the "uninitiated," Samhain was Glenn Danzig's band after the Misfits, formed immediately after the dissolution of the original group, carrying over the devilocks with even darker imagery. Samhain also played Misfits songs like "Death Comes Ripping" and "London Dungeon." The band included longtime Misfits photographer (and Doyle's high school classmate) Eerie Von, first on drums and later on bass. Samhain was the band Rick Rubin signed to Def Jam before they changed their name to Danzig. "Twist of Cain" and "Possession" by Danzig actually began as Samhain songs.

I bought some blood-red-colored acrylic paint at the craft store. At home, I took one of those "going tailgating at the football game" type coolers and filled it halfway with warm tap water from the sink. I figured that if I mixed the paint with water, it would be thin enough to run, and the color would then dry in the shape of the drips. Voila, blood show!

I mixed the paint into the water, dipped a kitchen spatula into the mixture, and then held it over my head, allowing the watery acrylic paint to drip down my hair, face, shoulders, arms, and torso. As I had hoped, it dried on my skin with that "dripping" look. Success.

It became the Black Veil Brides stage look for the first year or so of the original band.

Toward the end of my time in Cincinnati we had a show at the Mad Hatter in Covington, Kentucky. It was about four months before my eighteenth birthday. I'd forgotten to get the paint. Usually, I'd mix it up in the same cooler I'd always had and use that spatula to drip the watery blood-red acrylic paint all over the band and myself.

I didn't find any red paint at the nearest craft store, so I grabbed black. I figured that would look cool too. But the black paint just wouldn't mix quite right. It didn't drip, so it wouldn't dry that way, either. Instead, it sort of smeared onto our skin as it dried.

I stood and looked at it in a mirror for the first time. Around that period, there were different bands, maybe Eighteen Visions and Avenged Sevenfold, who'd crafted this "dirty" look. That sort of vibe where it looked like they'd just climbed out of the grave. It didn't look the same as that. I thought, "This is actually way cooler. If I come up with different designs, we can even have unique patterns for each member."

As I moved away from the water and started to work with just the paint, I liked the "sleekness" we could achieve. We shaped and designed it. Later, as the definitive incarnation of the band formed in LA, I experimented with different designs for myself.

I never wanted to do the all-white face thing, but I always aspired to more than just eyeliner. I liked the idea of these dramatic visages. The "war paint" became an extension of the characters we'd created, and each individual chose a readily identifiable design of his own to match the look of his face. The acrylic paint became the most efficient method to achieve the exact image we craved.

There weren't other options available to us, anyway. Body paint would run in a certain way that didn't look right. It smudged all over the place. I did try contacting the people at Mehron, who make professional performance and theatrical makeup, the kind of stuff one might find at the local Halloween store or year-round costume shop. It was a lofty proposition at the time, but I suggested that it would be a good idea to get in on the "ground floor" with us. We could develop a Black Veil Brides palette with them. Supply us with some free or heavily discounted makeup, and we'll promote it as we get bigger.

To their credit, they wound up becoming the first company to sponsor us. They sent over all kinds of makeup, but unfortunately, it just never worked the right way for our purposes. They sent us water-soluble stuff, which just meant we'd sweat it off over time.

As the years went on, we never did anything the "correct" way. We didn't use the technique where baby powder combined with body heat will "set" the makeup. We'd established a specific look we could only manage with paint. That stuff is like glue. It stuck to our body hair and hurt like crazy to peel off. It left a mess everywhere we went.

As CC often pointed out, our hotel rooms looked like crime scenes after we woke up from the black paint smeared all over the sheets. (Those poor hotel housekeepers.)

The paint took its place as one of the weapons in my arsenal. Two of the big "breaks" in my career incorporated that paint. The first was the T-shirt with my face on it that for a time outsold the *Twilight* merch at Hot Topic. The second, of course, was the music video for "Knives and Pens."

14

KNIVES & PENS

I turned eighteen on December 26, 2008.

I moved to Los Angeles, just as I'd planned for nearly as long as I could remember.

My girlfriend had come to Cincinnati to spend Christmas with me and my family before the move. When my mom drove us to the airport, I told her, "Don't worry, I'm coming back home in a few weeks." But she knew that wasn't true. She could sense it.

"You're not coming back in a few weeks," she said with a faint smile. "But that's okay."

I had that bit of money from the Montana Meth Project and AT&T commercials, and I was dating someone whose career was growing steadily. There's less than a slim chance

I'd have made it in California as long as I did without my ex-girlfriend's financial support.

She and I had a very serious relationship that frankly we just weren't ready to have. We shared a one-bedroom apartment, with our dog and two cats, with the responsibilities of much older people, in one of the most expensive places to live in the United States.

I had just turned eighteen, and she was less than two years older than me. She paid for the apartment while I did my best to keep it clean and whatever else I could do to feel like I was earning my keep while earning absolutely no income to share with her.

Right after I got to LA, my girlfriend got word that the sequel to the *Halloween* remake was moving forward with a three-month shoot in Covington, Georgia, scheduled to begin in late February 2009. I didn't see that I had any choice other than to accompany her there. What was I going to do, stay in Hollywood by myself? Remember, we were teenagers in love. Plus, I wanted to visit a film set! Who wouldn't want to do that?

Of course, I never intended to stay for the *entire* production. My original plan was to go for a short time and then return to California and resume work on Black Veil Brides.

I stepped out of the airport in Georgia and realized I'd left my wallet on the plane. I hadn't been in town long enough to get a California driver's license, and my wallet had my Ohio identification in it. When we learned it would take up to eight weeks to receive a new ID, I began to accept I'd be in Georgia for the duration of the *Halloween II* shoot.

There is absolutely nothing glamorous about sitting on a movie set all day, every day, without an actual job to do. It can be tedious and boring for someone who *has* a legitimate reason to be there, let alone someone who is sitting around doing nothing.

Covington is a small town about thirty-five miles east of Atlanta with nothing to do in it. And without a driver's license, I had no real means of getting myself around town, anyway. So I'd sit holding my girlfriend's purse while people always asked why I was there.

I was this eighteen-year-old goth-looking kid wandering around the set every day and in the way all of the time. I'd hang out at craft service and eat a bunch of food. Anytime someone would ask me who I was, I'd try to explain to him or her, "Well, I'm in a *band*..."

Tyler Mane, the former professional wrestler who took on the mantle of Michael Myers in the rebooted franchise, was always very pleasant to me, as was his wife, Renae.

As for Rob Zombie, the weight of the movie was on his shoulders already. I'm sure he wasn't thrilled to have the eighteen-year-old boyfriend of his lead actress loitering on his set.

Malcolm McDowell, star of cinema classics *A Clockwork Orange* (1971) and *Caligula* (1979), played Dr. Loomis in the *Halloween* remake and its sequel. We chatted a bit. (Scout and I even grabbed lunch with him once, a few months after the movie wrapped.)

Years later, when we made *American Satan* together, Malcolm didn't recognize me. Why would I remind him? He never did put two and two together, and I don't blame him.

THEY DON'T NEED TO UNDERSTAND

Regularly, I found myself in situations like the time executives from Dimension Films (the company responsible for *The Crow* and *Scream*) crowded around a laptop to watch an edit of the first trailer. There I was, trying to get through on my way back from craft service because there was no other pathway to get around. I stood there, hair in my face, holding my stupid bagel, now a silent "participant" in this professional conversation.

I kept telling everyone I was in a "band" because I didn't have anything else to say for myself. Scout kept saying, "You should tell Rob's manager about your band. Maybe he could manage you!" Her encouragement was lovely, of course. But the situation was not ideal. I'd burned a couple of CDs at the Holiday Inn Express in Covington with the demos for "Knives and Pens" and "The Gunsling" on them. Rob's then-manager, Andy, was kind enough to give them a listen one day. (Rob even wandered over to check it out, too.)

After a polite listen, they were cordial about the songs, but they didn't seem too impressed. Admittedly the recordings themselves were pretty rough, though I should point out that the recording of "Knives and Pens" they heard on the set that day is the same version later used in the music video, which has amassed 125 million views since it was posted on YouTube the same year Rob Zombie's *Halloween II* was released.

Speaking of the "Knives and Pens" video (and music videos in general), there was one thing that made everything about that three-month stay on the set completely worth it.

I saw this guy shooting behind-the-scenes b-roll, presumably for publicity materials or the eventual DVD release. He walked around wearing this Detroit Tigers hat, just like the one Tom Selleck wore on TV as *Magnum P.I.* in the eighties. He even had the mustache. I didn't know his name, so I nicknamed him "Magnum P.I." in my mind.

This man was budding music video director Patrick Fogarty. We became fast friends on set, and as anyone who has followed my work knows, we've collaborated ever since.

After we'd all returned to LA, Patrick called me up one day. "Let's get a music video together for your band. I know you don't have a lot of money to spend. If you can come up with a couple of grand, I'd love to shoot something with you as soon as next week."

I was available because I was always "available." But I didn't actually have a *band*. Nobody from back home had followed me to California. I had every intention of building a new version of Black Veil Brides, but I had yet to find anyone to join it at that point.

My ex introduced me to a drummer named Sandra Alva. Plus, I'd heard a guitarist named Chris Bluser, whom I'd met in Ohio, had relocated to Riverside.

So I knew two people who were both living in Southern California and who could play instruments, or at the very least, could pretend to play them in a music video. But I still needed a bass player. I scoured the ad section on MySpace, where I found a kid named Alan. So, this would be the new Black Veil Brides: Sandra, Chris, Alan, and me.

Sandra had a steady job at the time, so I convinced her to help fund the music video with the promise that I would repay her ASAP. My parents loaned me some money, too. (All of them were paid back pretty quickly, by the way.)

We soon had the two thousand dollars Pat needed to make this video.

Patrick and I wrote the narrative storyline interspersed with performance footage. We held some rudimentary auditions to cast the main character and the bullies who torment him. We used Sandra's girlfriend's house for exterior shots and then did the interior scenes on location at the apartment I shared with my girlfriend.

For the performance footage, we rented some space at Atomic Studios on Olympic Boulevard in downtown Los Angeles, a reliable location with cheap rates on the outskirts of the city, near a diaper factory. Atomic maintained a stockroom full of old props, so I grabbed some headless mannequins, which we used as set decoration.

It was important to me that our first music video had something to say. I'd followed the case of the West Memphis Three and the efforts to free them. These were the three Arkansas teens imprisoned for the grisly murder of three young boys, a conviction seemingly based on little "evidence" other than the fact that they wore black clothing, listened to heavy metal music, and similar circumstantial nonsense. No DNA results tied them to the murders. The "WM3" was the subject of several documentaries. They garnered support from public figures like Eddie Vedder, Henry Rollins, and Metallica, who began a long working relationship with the directors of *Paradise Lost: The Child Murders at Robin Hood Hills* and its two follow-up sequels. The WM3 were finally released in 2011.

The "Knives and Pens" video began with a sound bite from the case, where "young people involved with the occult" are described as "wearing black fingernails, having their hair painted black, wearing black T-shirts; sometimes they will tattoo themselves..."

I had the idea for us to proudly wear all *white* in the video, which fit thematically.

We were all set to start shooting when suddenly Alan was on his phone, crying. His girlfriend's dog had died. Alan left for San Jose to comfort her, and I never saw or heard from him again. But even with only a drummer and a single guitarist, I was determined to make the video happen. We'd come too far to let one guy's absence derail it.

To fill the space left by Alan, we grabbed this big lightbox that happened to be in the studio and went about filming our performances.

Patrick did a monumental favor for me and delivered an incredible video. It was particularly gratifying after so many years of different incarnations that failed to measure up to how I'd always envisioned Black Veil Brides should be. It captured how Black Veil Brides should be presented and set the tone for what was ahead.

Aside from a person at Roadrunner Records who asked for a press kit then never contacted me again after I sent it, the industry continued to ignore Black Veil Brides. One booking agent who handled many of the major acts in the

Warped Tour scene flatly dismissed us because, as he put it, "It's not 1984. Nobody wants this."

But people outside of the music business connected with "Knives and Pens" in a massive way. After we uploaded the video to YouTube, it had nearly half a million views within a matter of days. It had ten million views before our first album, *We Stitch These Wounds*, was even released.

People asked me countless times to explain exactly how that happened, what secrets I can reveal to replicate the kind of buzz that sends a video well past one hundred million plays. I wish I had the blueprint stashed in a drawer. If I did, I'd make sure every Black Veil Brides, Andy Black, and Juliet Simms clip got there and all of my friends' videos, too.

History was rewritten in a way that gives me more credit as a "MySpace celebrity" than I was. I had a modest following. It was the equivalent to the level of influence someone with ten thousand Twitter followers might have now. It wasn't enough to explain "Knives and Pens."

I'd like to think the answer lies in my determined optimism that there were other people out there who would connect with how I felt, what the video conveyed, how the song sounded, and the authenticity and earnestness with which it was created and delivered.

I don't know why it took off or why it's continued to find an audience every year since it was released. But I am confident we owe much of what came next to "Knives and Pens."

15

MEALS & DEALS

ONCE THERE WAS SOME genuine momentum happening around the "Knives and Pens" video, it became ever more urgent for me to put a real band together to back it up.

Around the same time that Ashley Purdy joined, we met guitarist David Burton, a.k.a. "Pan," who moved to LA from Chicago. Pan's time with the band was brief, but he was instrumental in the evolution of the visual/image element. Plus, he introduced us to Jinxx.

It wasn't long after the lineup of Sandra, Chris, Ashley, Pan, and I came together that a small indie label called Standby contacted the band via MySpace. Neil, the owner, knew about the earlier incarnations but wasn't impressed with the Ohio based lineups.

About a year after he'd initially dismissed the early BVB, his fourteen-year-old daughter came home one day and told him about the "Knives and Pens" video. He did a bit of homework and decided to contact the band. My dad and I both spoke to him a bit.

YouTube numbers didn't matter to people in the music industry back then, certainly not the way they do now. But Standby sent us a record contract. Nobody else had done that.

We were happy to sign with anyone. We read the contract, but we never hired a lawyer. None of us understood what we were reading. (Anyone reading this book with plans to sign anything: hire an attorney first.)

In the late summer of 2009, Richard Villa III became an important character in my life, thanks in no small part to Sandra Alva. A former student at the Otis College of Art and Design, Richard is an artist, illustrator, creative director, and graphic designer, as well as the owner and curator at Exhibit A Gallery, which he opened in 2008 with professional skateboarding legend Tony Alva. Exhibit A was looking for a band to perform at an upcoming event. Sandra heard about it and suggested Black Veil Brides.

Richard watched the "Knives and Pens" video and said that he'd like to meet with us. A few of us went down to Richard's gallery. He and I immediately hit it off. We talked about music and religion on that first day—all of the things we continued to talk about for years.

The "Bipolar" art show opening reception had food, drinks, and an ex-member of Danzig as the DJ. It was increasingly clear that we weren't going to get added to any other shows in Los Angeles. It was our first real opportunity to perform in my adopted city.

I started spending a lot of time at the gallery. When I didn't have anything to eat, Richard would loan me enough cash to get a piece of pizza across the street. I'd take my slice back to the gallery, and we'd sit and talk about God, the devil, music, and art.

Now that I'd started to taste a *small* bit of success, I began to see myself as less dependent on my then-girlfriend. I knew we shouldn't live together much longer either way. We would often argue, as young couples do. For all of my maturity, when it came to art and creative drive, I was still a kid when it came to matters of the heart.

In the early days of Black Veil Brides making records and touring, I'd come home from tour, and my ex and I would briefly reconcile, then break up again. It went like that for some time, the on-again/off-again relationship many of us experience when we are very young.

I still had a few grand in the bank, which in Los Angeles wouldn't pay the rent for more than a month or two at best. I didn't have any credit or a steady income.

I briefly stayed with one of the guys from the band before I decided to just live in my car.

I eventually burned through most of my cash but refused to surrender. Even during periods when my ex and I were back together, I'd visit her in her lovely home in the valley and pretend everything was okay, even when I was sleeping in my car or paying someone to let me sleep on their floor for a week or two. I needed to establish myself, stand on my own feet. As miserable as it was to live in my car for as long as I did, it made me hungrier.

I couldn't keep parking in the K-Mart parking lot overnight for very long because people knocked on the windows early in the morning and told me to leave. It wasn't practical to park in random places on the street either as there was the danger of getting towed.

As I was still trying to cement a real lineup for Black Veil Brides, it dawned on me that perhaps I should start parking my car somewhere musicians hung out.

I took what remained of my savings from the Montana Meth Project PSAs and pooled it with whatever cash the existing band members could put together. We rented a "lockout" room at a place in the San Fernando Valley called ABC Rehearsal Studio.

Rehearsal lockouts are relatively cheap and usually open twenty-four hours with people coming in and out constantly. They all have pretty strict rules against people living inside of them, which they will enforce, but I figured I could park my car there and sleep in it without much hassle from anybody, so long as I wasn't trying to sleep overnight in the actual space. So, I'd doze off in my car at this place in North Hollywood, wake up in the morning, walk the halls, work on Black Veil Brides songs, and try to make a real band.

I didn't plan for this to be more than an extremely temporary living situation, but it sort of snowballed into a much more extended time than I'd anticipated.

My daily food intake usually consisted of Junior Mints and energy drinks. The floors of my '98 Cadillac were stacked nearly to the seats with empty cans and candy boxes. Junior Mints were my favorite confectionary as a kid. As a young adult with little education and no money, it seemed like a great idea to turn them into my regular "meal" of choice.

It was at ABC Rehearsal Studio where I met my first LA rock star, ex-W.A.S.P. guitarist and solo artist, Chris Holmes. He was the first guy that I'd grown up seeing in music videos and listening to on records that I met in California. He'd often park his Trans-Am next to my Cadillac and show me these crazy guitars he made from tree stumps. He also brought me giant bags of ice. He was a genuinely sweet and friendly guy.

I know his solo project is called Mean Man and that scene in the 1989 documentary *Decline of Western Civilization Part II: The Metal Years*, where he's floating in a swimming pool swilling vodka as his mom sits poolside, is the stuff of rock 'n' roll myth. But he was extremely welcoming, charming, and friendly, with nothing to gain from it. He was very complimentary to Black Veil Brides when he'd pop in to hear us rehearse.

It was a hassle trying to keep my car going. The Cadillac would sometimes turn itself on in the middle of the night. The horn somehow became permanently engaged, which meant that anytime I started the car, the horn would blare the entire time I drove somewhere until I parked and cut the engine or until the battery died, whichever came first.

It seemed like things were looking up for us professionally when we secured a manager, but he only stuck with us for about two weeks. At some point early on, he read the record contract we'd signed and taken a few of us to dinner at Universal CityWalk, where he explained that there would be nothing he or anyone else could do for us because the contract we'd signed was simply too terrible.

Was it that awful? We left pretty demoralized but determined to figure something out.

A friend of one of the guys, who worked for Mötley Crüe, suggested we have the Crüe's lawyer take a look at the contract for us. We were able to secure a meeting. That attorney, Dina LaPolt, said I reminded her of Cher. We went to meetings in full gear back then; she still cracks jokes about how we'd leave black paint all over her office furniture. She took an immediate liking to us and offered to help the band out however she could.

Dina confirmed what we'd now suspected, which was that our contract sucked. But the situation wasn't insurmountable or even really uncommon. Bands often sign deals that are less than favorable to them. It's not always as cut and dried as "evil record label vs. artist." Labels risk overextending themselves for bands that could very well go nowhere.

It's a credit to Dina, Neil, and the attorneys at Universal that a pleasant way to let us graduate to a more prominent label was determined, with the Standby logo still on our CDs.

Ash Avildsen became our first booking agent. Ash had moved to Los Angeles to pursue his dreams in the entertainment business as an agent, an indie record label owner, and eventually, a filmmaker. He got behind me as a friend and supporter very early on.

We told Ash that we had an attorney, but we needed management, so he reached out to a handful of managers on our behalf. One of them was Rob "Blasko" Nicholson.

Blasko began his career as bassist for early crossover/ thrash band Cryptic Slaughter. At one point he was a member of Danzig, then the bassist for Rob Zombie, recording and touring behind *Hellbilly Deluxe*, *The Sinister Urge*, and *Educated Horses*. After a successful audition in 2003, he joined Ozzy Osbourne's band.

Blasko's newly launched management firm shared office space with Sumerian Records, the label owned by Ash, who introduced us via email. I'd just returned from the set of *Halloween II* a few months prior, so of course in my reply I said something like, "Hey, Blasko! You used to play with Rob Zombie. I sort of know Rob Zombie?"

I arrived covered in dust and soot the first time we met. My Cadillac had broken down on the way to the meeting. Smoke rose from under the hood. My ex sat in the driver's seat while I pushed the car into a Goodwill parking lot, then we walked the rest of the way.

I think Blasko got a kick out of me. My relentless drive and intense self-belief in my plans and vision amused him. I saw him as a kindred spirit and mentor. (Years later, Juliet and I asked him to officiate our wedding. He graciously accepted.)

Of course, not to toot my own horn, but it wasn't difficult to get behind the idea of "me," considering I'd put so much of it in place already. After years without anyone in the industry having my back, I had support from this bulldog of an attorney, Dina, who was willing to fight for me; a booking agent who aggressively made a case for us to promoters; and now Blasko, himself a musician who'd been there. It was validating.

Of course, even the best in the business can't guarantee a band will earn any fans.

That was still up to us.

16

CARS & GUITARS

At some point in 2009, Chris Hollywood was out, which meant we needed a second guitarist. Pan's old band in Chicago had once opened for a group called The Dreaming. He remembered that band's guitarist and suggested we draft him to fill the vacant spot.

Jinxx joined BVB about a month after the Exhibit A performance. He quickly took to calling me his little brother, and I know that's something he took to heart. He's tremendously wise with a unique soulfulness that I've always much appreciated. He's been there for me in so many situations, as a musician and friend. He even opened his home to me at a time when I had nowhere else to go. I'm reasonably sure he can play every instrument in the known universe and play them all with unmatched style and showmanship.

Honestly, Jinxx has all sorts of skills. One night I pulled over and discovered there was a small fire burning in my engine. I called Jinxx, and he drove down and did some kind of voodoo that allowed me to get the rest of the way to wherever I was going.

By November of that year, we had decided to replace Pan. Jinxx spoke highly of his friend Jake Pitts. From the very first time I met him at his old apartment, he was always perfecting his playing and songwriting, as well as his ability to engineer and produce music. Jake is by far one of the most dedicated musicians I have or will ever know.

In those early days, we forged a bond that few people are lucky enough to share, a friendship that deepened as we continued. He's remained kind and ready to take on anything. In more recent years, after the sudden and tragic death of his mother, Jake dedicated himself to a healthier and more positive lifestyle, which was truly inspiring.

We embarked on our first tour in December 2009, with about twenty shows booked around the country. We traveled in two vehicles, certainly not meant for touring: an SUV and my dad's Chevy HHR, which was Chevy's version of the Chrysler PT Cruiser.

I planned on trying to find a real place to live once we returned. Part of the sales pitch to get Jake to join the band was inviting him to come and live with me after the tour.

I was confident I'd have a place by then. Jake had just taken a job at a Verizon Wireless call center, and we had a hard time telling him, "Hey, quit your job, come on tour, and lose your apartment!" I told him he could come and live with me for free. I needed someone who could play guitar and record, so it seemed like a fair enough trade.

My dad worked as our tour manager, merch guy, lighting tech—he was everything.

We had these floodlights we bought at Home Depot and spray painted black. We set them up on either side behind the stage and hooked them up to a power strip, which controlled the lights. So there were only two settings for that "light show": on and off. My dad learned the songs well enough to flip the lights on and off in synchronicity with the music. We'd gotten these big dead bride figures from a Halloween store and customized them with paint. (One of these is in the music video for "The Vengeance.") All of the homemade staging went into my dad's car.

The merchandise and gear were divided between the vehicles, as well. The SUV had a hatch in the back and four seats in which to shove ourselves. My legs are long, so when we slept at night, I'd have to roll the windows down and hang my feet out of the car. It was the middle of winter, so I'd cover my feet in multiple pairs of socks.

To start the tour, we drove straight from California to Cincinnati in two or three days, with only a few brief stops on the way. After we regrouped at my parents' house, we made the drive to Cleveland and debuted the new incarnation of Black Veil Brides to the world at Peabody's Concert Club, a semi-legendary venue that ended its thirty-year run in 2013.

It was so early on that I think I even did Jake's makeup for him before the show, like someone painting a kid's face at a school carnival. When we saw there were 150 people there to see us, we realized how much the "Knives and Pens" video was connecting with people around the country. The momentum seemed almost tangible.

Not every show was like that kickoff in Cleveland. I remember one night where fewer than five people showed up. All of them were there because they were fans of Jinxx's previous band. (Maybe one of them had seen the music video for "Knives and Pens.")

We finished in Southern California with a pair of shows that gave us each a sense of pride and accomplishment. We played to five hundred people at the Whisky a Go Go, the Sunset Strip rock club that served as an early proving ground for Van Halen and Guns N' Roses. The next night we sold out Chain Reaction in Anaheim, the venue memorialized in the Bleeding Through DVD as "the CBGBs of the West Coast."

My take-home pay from the tour was about six hundred bucks, and frankly, I was thrilled. It was the first money I'd ever made from music.

My dad traveled back with us to Los Angeles, where I had been staying on Jinxx's couch. My '98 Cadillac El Dorado had stopped working, so I'd parked it in front of my girlfriend's house and just left it there. It was pretty much done. I couldn't get it to move. I didn't know what else to do with it, and I didn't have the money to get it fixed.

In California, my dad saw firsthand that his son was subsisting on Junior Mints, energy drinks, and pizza from

7-Eleven. It didn't take long for him to insist on helping me secure a real place to live (plus, I'd already promised Jake he could live with me for free).

My only means of transportation, which doubled as my "home," sat lifeless on the street in Burbank, collecting more than a dozen citations. Incredibly, it was never towed. The first order of business was to have my Cadillac relocated to a service station. My dad was instrumental in making that happen. He made sure a 76 station fixed it up well.

I didn't have any credit or steady employment, so my dad offered to cosign for whatever we could find, any sort of place that could deal in cash and would allow us to live month-to-month.

We found a place across the street from this big, old, Victorian-style home that housed the comedic rock band Green Jellÿ (formerly known as Green Jellö), who had a hit in the early nineties with "Three Little Pigs," which featured guest vocals from Tool's Maynard Keenan. The place is rather famous among Tool fans, as Tool and A Perfect Circle recorded there. Many of the Green Jellÿ and Tool music videos were filmed there, as well. Tool drummer Danny Carey was in Green Jellÿ from 1989–1994. (I'm pretty sure the place is visible in a sketch on HBO's *Mr. Show*, which I loved.).

It was a street-level one-bedroom apartment with one little extra room adjacent to the kitchen. The bathroom was like the cabin-style bathrooms on a cruise ship or ferry.

December 23, the day after he cosigned the lease for my tiny apartment, my dad got in his Chevy HHR and headed back East, racing to make it home to Cincinnati in time for Christmas. As he drove through Texas, in the middle of a whiteout snowstorm, a semitruck hit my dad's car, sending him crashing through the windshield.

He lay in the snow on the side of the road for hours before anyone discovered him. A helicopter airlifted him to a hospital in Amarillo. I was shaken by it, of course, but by the time I got the news, he was resting safely. I'm so glad he escaped from that harrowing accident in one piece and with no significant injuries, or worse. It's crazy to think that all happened on the same day I moved into my first apartment of my own.

It was a place we nicknamed the Compound. And it was ridiculous.

17

COKE & VOMIT

SANDRA'S SOCIAL NETWORK CAME to my rescue once again. It was thanks to her that I was able to find a roommate who could help me cover the rent at the Compound.

Jessica was a girl from Pennsylvania who dated Sandra and agreed to relocate to Hollywood after our first tour so they could be together. But by the time the tour finished, they had broken up. Jessica had only recently come out to her parents and was eager to get her life moving on the West Coast regardless, so she came to California anyway.

My new roommate became sick with food poisoning right away. We hadn't realized we needed to have the electric bill switched over to us before we moved in, so there we sat, at Christmastime, with the lights off. My dad had narrowly escaped a near-death experience just after helping me secure that apartment. Next thing I knew, it was New Year's Eve, and I lie down, kept awake by the sound of poor Jessica throwing up.

By no means would she be the only person to vomit into the Compound's toilet.

The first time I ever got drunk was in that apartment. Every other time I'd had alcohol, it was maybe half a shot, and then I would just pretend I was inebriated. I tried vodka for the first time there; it was the first time I was ever totally obliterated.

Jessica, Jake, and I were regularly joined in our tiny apartment by the rest of the band. Many celebratory nights (and shameful mornings) at the Compound included a rogue's gallery of struggling LA musicians and an assortment of significant others.

A nearby Rite Aid drugstore became our dealer of choice for any alcohol we could afford once we'd scraped together a few dollars from whatever collection of people came over on a given night. We drank a lot of Seagram's 7. We consumed so much of it that a bunch of us went out and got tattoos of the Seagram's 7 logo. I put that logo on my flesh twice. One has the words "American Rock N' Roll" surrounding it, the other features a tiny koala (dressed as me) drinking a bottle of Seagram's 7.

A German musician named Romeo showed up at the door one day and asked if he could stay for a bit because he knew someone we knew. (It turned out he had been staying with this girl, and she'd kicked him out.) At this point, the people who lived at the Compound were Jake, Jessica, this total stranger from Europe with a thick German accent, and me. It was all four of us in this one-bedroom place that was barely any bigger than a studio apartment with constant overnight guests.

For a year or two, the place became so disgusting and destroyed that it became infamous amongst the LA rock scene. I believe Jinxx came up with the name "The Compound," a moniker we chose to embrace to the fullest extent possible.

One night we decided to redecorate with as much junk furniture as we could find on the streets. We wound up with four couches in one room and a bunch of giant televisions from the eighties that didn't work. I don't know how we managed to carry those inside.

We'd hand black acrylic paint to visitors and ask them to put whatever they wanted on the walls. There were obscenities from the floor to the ceiling. The Compound looked less like an apartment and more like a sketchy rock club's disgusting dressing room.

The first time the band received a check for any significant amount of money, we decided we'd splurge on two fifths of our most coveted alcoholic dream: a new variation of Jack Daniels called Gentlemen Jack, marketed as an "elevated" whiskey. "What's it going to be like?" It turned out to be the same stuff, as far as I could tell, disguised in a different bottle. I was disappointed. We got wasted anyway, but I argued with Jake about Gentleman Jack. He was convinced it was special.

The Compound was where I learned that I shouldn't drink rum. A billboard near the apartment advertised Sailor Jerry Spiced Rum with a slogan that said something like "Make New Friends." After swallowing an entire bottle's worth by myself, I started telling everyone they should change their slogan to "Fight Your Friends!"

Drunk on rum one evening, I became angry for no discernable reason, like Incredible Hulk level pissed off. I smashed all of the lights in the apartment with my fists. Eventually, I ran outside into the street and in a fit of rage I grabbed this heavy, ornate-looking, graveyard-type metal tip from the top of a fence and somehow snapped it clean off.

I woke up the next morning and discovered the bits of iron fence in my bed. I swore off rum after that. It was voluntary abstinence but only from one specific type of alcohol.

I went with Matt Good (who briefly lived at the Compound) to Target around Halloween one year, where we saw this dog costume with a bunch of grapes attached to its back. We thought it was hysterical, so we painted a picture of it across an entire wall of the apartment and scrawled "Grape Dog" next to it. A whole wall was just Grape Dog.

Every night was a party. We'd invite five people over, and each of them would ask someone else till suddenly there were a hundred people. It was such a madhouse so often that at one point, my future wife came and went without her and I even meeting each other.

Eventually, there were so many people crashing there at the same time that I stopped sleeping there myself as often as possible despite the fact I paid half the rent.

As someone troubled by persistent worries and fears for so many years, this was a moment in time where I started to feel fearless and even somewhat carefree. It was as if nothing could genuinely hurt me. Of course, looking back, I know that I was simply burying all of that anxiety, ignoring or numbing my worries, or crudely masking my fears.

Toward the end of our time there, things got a bit darker. As the drinking stretched further into the daylight, until people were drunk during all hours of the day and night, I encountered other substances. I tried acid and molly, but none of those things did anything for me. It didn't work. Whenever I've tried to smoke weed, I've thrown up.

At some point, I heard that the best prevention against blacking out or getting the spins was to do a little bit of cocaine. I heard that it would reset a person back to zero or give a new wave of energy, which would make it easier to continue drinking even more.

The whole idea of cocaine is hilarious to me. For starters, it tastes terrible. The headaches, sore throat, and diarrhea aren't my idea of glamorous. Coke makes a person feel like they have to say everything they are thinking and at a pace that makes it nearly incomprehensible. "Hey, hurry up and finish talking, so I can talk some more!"

Next comes the sleeplessness. What's the fun in all of that? I don't see it.

Thankfully I never fell into any sort of routine with drugs. For better or worse, booze was my thing. When people ask, "Don't you miss partying?" I wonder why. I sort of did everything.

It's incredible nothing truly awful ever happened to us at the Compound.

There wasn't anybody around in those days trying to take advantage of us. We didn't have strangers contriving compromising situations so they could gossip about us. We were free to get silly without embarrassment. We weren't in a huge band; we were just those guys in eyeliner who had a place where people could come and get crazy.

The vast majority of my memories of the place are about grabbing liquor at Rite Aid, sitting around talking about how we'd become the biggest band in the world, and then having all of these different colorful characters showing up to party every night.

The partying was whatever to me. The mission remained my utmost priority.

18

MERCH & MAJORS

"KNIVES AND PENS" CONTINUED to kick down doors for us. The "buzz" became so loud that Hot Topic took notice, and before long, two more significant people entered my life.

The music Jake and Jinxx were writing was headed in a heavier and more traditionally metal direction. This style required a different skillset in the drum department, and Sandra came from a more punk and emo-rock background. We connected on a shared love of bands like Alkaline Trio. She and I would drive around listening to Tegan and Sara.

The guitar players knew Christian "CC" Coma from another project they had done together. His style was much more in line with the type of stuff we were writing.

A few of us met up with Sandra at a Starbucks in Burbank to talk it over. She wanted something different from Black Veil Brides than what we wanted. There were no hard feelings. It was a seamless transition, and Sandra has been a friend of the band ever since. My attitude at the time was always about solving the next problem, to keep this thing moving forward, but the situation with Sandra wasn't that way. She was very gracious.

CC is and will always be one of the most joyful and genuinely lovely people I have had the pleasure to spend time around. He's someone who can pick me up when I am down and put a smile on the face of just about everyone he meets. He can adapt to any situation. For example, when he joined Black Veil Brides, he went gung-ho into the uniform style we'd devised with the makeup and stage clothes. (Jinxx even Photoshopped a picture of him to see what he'd look like as one of us after he'd impressed us with his musical ability at his audition. We could see it was going to work.)

CC was eager to be involved with the crazy hair and everything else. In the early days, I encountered so many people who were into joining the band but were insistent about maintaining their own "look." I'd often think, "Cool, you have your style. How's that working out for you so far?" CC understood what we were trying to project, and he shared our adoration for bands that presented something unique and specific onstage.

Not only did he contribute to the overall visual vibe, but he also developed his persona within those parameters, solidifying his place. It felt like he'd always been there with us.

He is an incredible drummer and an even better friend.

Standby Records was able to place a single Black Veil Brides shirt design onto the Hot Topic website. It was after our inaugural tour but before the release of our debut album. I remember going over the artwork, on my first smartphone, when I lived with Jinxx. We believed we had enough of a following from YouTube, MySpace, the clubs, and my original social media presence to be able to sell at least a little bit with Hot Topic. They promised to put the shirt in their physical stores if it did well enough online.

In those days, the e-commerce and retail sides, like many brands, were pretty different entities. The "brick and mortar" locations were limited in terms of space. By contrast, the webstore looked more like one of those Rockabillia advertisements in the back of *Hit Parader*, where I used to order shirts representing groups like the Damned. It seemed like every meaningful band, down to the most obscure, had a shirt on the Hot Topic site.

We kept it simple. The design was a distressed, high-contrast, black and white photo of my face, sporting an early prototype of the makeup, in white ink on a black shirt. The print was large and bold, intended to evoke the vibe of the classic Misfits "fiend" logo.

Following a successful "test run" on their website, Hot Topic put the shirt in a few of their Southern California stores. Rumor has it that it became the biggest selling shirt at the Hollywood and Highland location for a few weeks, outselling all of the major label artists. At that particular store, it even began to compete with *Twilight* merchandise.

The tour put us face to face with the kids who connected with "Knives and Pens." We'd successfully enlisted a manager, booking agent, and attorney in our cause. Hot Topic was onboard. Standby Records was eager to release some music to the masses.

We needed to make an album.

The label had a place where they liked to send bands, but it was in Cleveland. Groups would fly into town and record at the label owner's studio with his in-house engineer.

None of us wanted to do that, but there wasn't much of a budget to make a decent record in California. Thankfully, Blasko volunteered to produce the album himself, working together with producers/engineers/mixers Josh Newell and G. Preston Boebel.

The first album was recorded in March and April 2010 at Clear Lake Recording Studios in North Hollywood. No Doubt, Jimmy Eat World, and Steel Panther have made records there. It's not far from Circus Liquor, a Hollywood landmark seen in a lot of movies.

Blasko was the producer in the sense that he was the guy who would come into the room and offer his opinion. It's no fault of his, but it wasn't like a John Feldmann situation where he's there all day. He gave us the reins, the opportunity to make the kind of record I wanted to make, and the freedom to have the type of songs the guitar players wanted to write.

Clear Lake has various sized rooms inside; I recorded my vocals in what was more or less a closet. The engineers were fantastic guys whose standard rates we couldn't afford. They worked cheaply for us as a favor, so the schedules were crazy. Josh, for example, was working on a Linkin Park record at NRG Studios at the same time. They'd often contact me in the middle of the night, at a moment's notice, to come and track more vocals.

We Stitch These Wounds was a combination of a few things. It contained a lot of music that Jake and Jinxx had written before knowing me, so I put lyrics and phrasing to it. "We Stitch These Wounds" is a song that existed in a different iteration before the album; it just so happened that Jake and Jinxx had a song that sounded similar enough that I could sing my lyrics and melodies over it with only a few changes.

I don't have a lot of vivid memories of making *We Stitch These Wounds*, at least not the way you're "supposed" to remember the excitement of making your first record. The record was in service of the greater plan. I knew we didn't have the money to make it sound the way we wanted it. Most of what I remember was sitting around making plans. I'd get mixes back and think, "Eh, it's not that great, but we'll keep pushing forward."

I wrote some of the melodies on the fly because we didn't have enough songs ready. I was writing "Never Give In" as I was singing the lines, for example—lots of trial and error.

An ex-member who was gone before the recording said at one point that Black Veil Brides didn't have the "magic" or "story" a band is "supposed" to have at that stage. I remember thinking, "Well, I don't give a shit about that, because I imagine that in the future, there *will* be a story to this record." And I was right.

The story is that it was a young band who had an audience that was growing in the underground, on a small independent label with a limited budget, who did their best.

Hot Topic continued to make our shirt available in an increasing number of markets as things ramped up to our first significant support tour, opening for From First to Last.

Nearly every Hot Topic store offered that T-shirt. (It's never gone out of production.)

Blasko called us to say Warner Bros. was interested in Black Veil Brides. The album wasn't even out yet, and there was an invite to a meeting with a major record label, based on the strength of our Hot Topic T-shirt sales. I sat in the car before the meeting at Warner Bros. listening to *We Stitch These Wounds*, and I just knew it didn't sound right.

I was proud of the songs themselves, but I tried to put myself in the position of someone who had never heard the band before. "Does this record sound like what I intended, like the message I want to put out into the world?" Really from the moment we completed the record, it never sounded the way any of us wanted. It wasn't big enough.

It didn't sound like the statement we wanted to make.

It pissed me off, but it also strengthened our resolve to fight that much harder. "We'll show everybody that this record that nobody thought was worth spending any time on is going to succeed anyway, and then we'll move onto the next one, and it'll be bigger and better."

Particularly in the early years, it always felt like we were never the band that got the shiny things, all of the stuff that seemed to come so much more smoothly for our peers. If we wanted something done, we had to do it. We were never darlings of any kind of scene. Even after we had a record deal and started touring the world, we were still the only ones outside of the fanbase who believed in Black Veil Brides as strongly as we did. (And as time has gone on, that's proven to be one of the coolest things about this band.)

And then, the idea that we could move from a small indie label to a major like Warner, where My Chemical Romance and Avenged Sevenfold had smashed into the mainstream, was huge. Before we went into the meeting, we met up with Blasko at an El Torito restaurant that was across the street from the Warner offices. As a good manager should, Blasko cautioned us to remember that there was no guarantee we'd see an offer.

But I had already begun to feel that signing to a major label was now inevitable.

As I had been when playing hockey or doing the dramatic reading of "Dig Up Her Bones" for the SCPA drama department, I was determined to make a big impression. Everything I did then was heightened and exaggerated, from my look to my attitude. I told myself, "Get in there. Show them who you are." We walked into the meeting in full gear.

I sat down, put my boots up on a piano that belonged to Neil Young, and began the conversation with a blunt icebreaker: "So, what are you going to do for us, exactly?"

Unsurprisingly, that didn't go over well. Warner Bros. did not make a deal with us.

But something else was already brewing with an executive named Jason Flom.

Jason started at Atlantic Records, under the guidance of the late Ahmet Ertegun, where he was instrumental in the careers of Twisted Sister, Skid Row, and Stone Temple Pilots, among many other bands. After he sold his own Lava Records imprint, he became CEO of Virgin Records and eventually of the larger Capitol Music Group, where he signed Katy Perry. He reclaimed Lava Records in 2009, where he signed Lorde and Jessie J.

Jason was friendly with the Chief Music Officer at Hot Topic, who encouraged him to check out our band. After he watched the "Knives and Pens" video, he started contacting Dina with relentless determination. He knew we had met with Warner Bros. Records.

He took two of us to "dinner," where both of us skipped the food in favor of booze. Jason understood this to mean we were badass rock stars who subsisted on almost nothing but a steady diet of whiskey and cigarettes. But the reality was much less "cool."

He had taken us to a landmark Italian eatery in West Hollywood, and I simply didn't want anything on the menu. Around that time, if I couldn't order grilled chicken, I just wouldn't eat. I didn't know what to say in front of this famous record executive. I just sort of stammered, "Oh, um, well, I don't eat." I'd drawn a blank. I said, "I *just* drink."

The less-than-glamorous truth is that it was all awkward, nervous energy. But he filled in the blanks with his imagination and incorporated it into the mystique we'd been building.

It was good that Warner had sort of stolen Jason's thunder. I'd gotten all of my "wait a minute, this could happen!" anxiousness out of my system by the time we were negotiating with Lava Records (which was now a part of Universal Republic). It gave us an even temperament and a responsible mindset to make sure everything was stable.

Jason became such a believer in our band that he was unwavering in his pursuit to make a deal and finessed things with Dina and Standby in such a way that everyone felt optimistic about the future of Black Veil Brides and their role in what would happen.

With Jason Flom and Universal Music behind us, it was time to set the world on fire.

19

OUTCASTS & AGITATORS

GIVEN HIS YEARS OF experience and his strong reputation, Jason is well-connected in the business. He introduced us to producer Josh Abraham, who worked with Linkin Park, 30 Seconds to Mars, Velvet Revolver, Atreyu, and Slayer, among others. Most importantly to me, Josh delivered my favorite Alkaline Trio album, *Agony & Irony*. He produced our next album, together with Luke Walker, who had worked with him on Alkaline Trio and is also credited on albums from Korn, From First to Last, and Filter.

We entered The Pulse Recording Studios together in early 2011 to make what became our second full-length album and major-label debut, *Set the World on Fire*. Songs like "The Legacy," "Fallen Angels," and "Rebel Love Song" sounded much closer to how I'd imagined Black Veil Brides in my head as a little kid with big dreams in Cincinnati.

Set the World on Fire, with few exceptions, is comprised of songs written as instrumental pieces before I added lyrics or melodies. We dug through every demo Jake, Jinxx, and CC had made together. Very shreddy instrumentals. A lot of those tracks began as fully fleshed-out instrumental pieces before I'd ever heard them. (It wasn't until *Wretched and Divine* that we wrote all new material together from scratch.)

Set the World on Fire was our first shot at making something big, sonically. I read a lot about Mutt Lange, the multiplatinum producer behind iconic rock albums by AC/DC and Def Leppard, and the "wall of sound" approach to vocal harmonies. The "Legacy" chorus, it's almost comical; every possible note that *could* be in there as harmony *is* in there.

If you isolate the backup vocals on *Set the World on Fire* and the *Rebels* EP, you'll hear like a hundred versions of Luke Walker going at once. He has incredible range and tone. Later on, I was doing more harmonies, especially with John Feldmann, but on those recordings, it's all Luke in the background (much of which is just lost in the mix anyway).

I will confess that I have little personal connection to a handful of the songs on that album, as the lyrics were more of a reflection of what I thought someone in my position would say than who I was or how I felt. I was still very young, and I had some people around me who were more into the eighties Sunset Strip hair metal, so I started to lean into that. I mean, I wanted to be cool, I wanted to be interesting, I wanted to have a mystique about me.

While I do enjoy *Set the World on Fire* and it's an integral part of our story, the songs themselves, in many cases, hold less of a special place for me. By the time we got to the next record, I had a clear vision for what I wanted to say and how I wanted to say it.

The "go big or go home" mentality drove the image just as much as the music now. I instituted a patently ridiculous but inflexible rule: so long as we were making an official band appearance, we were *never* to show up without our signature look in full makeup

Our *Set the World on Fire* era likenesses were on us anywhere we arrived together so long as we were doing something on behalf of the band. My inflexibility created some bizarre situations. Let's say a tattoo magazine wanted to photograph us. What would we do then? We'd have to come up with a warpaint-free variation of the BVB costume.

I'm not complaining. It isn't hard to do something like that when you actively *want* to. We loved getting dressed up and putting on all of the paint. As I said many times back then, I'd only ever quit doing it when it stopped being fun for me. I have a vivid memory of a 2012 European tour where I started putting on less and less makeup every day. It disappeared from my hands and my arms until it was just a bit of paint underneath my chin and on my face. Of course, that looked strange, because I had this pale white face with bat wings under my eyes but no other makeup anywhere else. It didn't work.

My point is, once I fell out of love with doing it, it was no longer genuine, so we stopped.

But during the era when we loved doing it, we were fully committed, no matter how crazy it was to pull together in different circumstances, even during the touring in support of the first album. Like the time we booked an appearance on Cincinnati radio to play "Knives and Pens" acoustically. It was during the August 2010 Sacred Ceremony Tour. They wanted us during the morning drive time, which meant "Andy Sixx" at six in the morning.

We played a show in Detroit and then drove all night to my parents' house, without sleeping. By the time we arrived, we just started reapplying our paint. Keep in mind nobody was *filming* us for this. It was radio, not television. But we wanted to make an impression on everyone at that station. And on anybody who chose to snap a photo. We wanted to look like Black Veil Brides when we arrived and throughout our visit.

In some respects, we were kind of jerks about it. We found it funny to be as obnoxious as possible. We knew it'd be a conversation starter. In the mind of this Gene Simmons and Paul Stanley disciple, rolling into a radio station looking like that might lead to more coverage. The makeup was as much a promotional tactic as it was our warpaint.

I was acutely aware of the fact that I was nineteen and in a bit of a pose as someone else. I was never entirely comfortable with myself in those days. It made it a hell of a lot easier to feel like somebody else when I looked in the mirror and couldn't see an inch of myself.

When you're covered head to toe in any kind of costume, it's a lot easier to escape yourself. Get dressed up for Halloween, and by the end of the night, most people find their mannerisms have changed, at least slightly. A big crazy tiger suit can get somebody puffing out their chest, making weird sounds, or doing stuff with their hands.

Remember, as a kid, I walked around the neighborhood dressed up as Batman. I wasn't roleplaying or engaged in some kind of game because I didn't have any friends. I did it because it made me feel cool. It made me feel like more than a milquetoast, run-of-the-mill nobody. I felt like a superhero. It didn't matter if other people understood.

One time when I was out as Batman, a group of bullies started hassling me. I escaped by telling them I'd get my cousin Alex to come and beat them up if they hurt me. I rushed home and told my dad about it. I was seven or eight years old and fully expected him to rise to my defense. I thought he'd find those bullies and teach them a lesson.

I was shocked that he simply wanted to have a conversation with me instead. It was crushing. I couldn't believe it! He explained to me that any kid walking around in public dressed like a superhero on any day that isn't Halloween is probably going to run into trouble. I was mad at his response at first, but I eventually understood his lesson.

I didn't dress like Batman anymore, but I was out in the world as a sort of superhero. I knew that walking into a radio station in costume at six in the morning would likely result in people reacting negatively toward us. But instead of getting mad about it, as I did as a little kid, I embraced it. It was exciting to compel people to talk about how we looked. They'd undoubtedly ask us about it on the air, which would buy us some more time to promote the band overall.

The motivation to prove myself to enemies both real and imagined, be they the people who dismissed me at school or who doctored photos on message boards, continued to propel me through these situations. I wanted my revenge. I was going into battle anytime we went anywhere. My veil, as it were, was this crazy-looking tough exterior, prepared to stand up against any backlash we might encounter for being who we wanted to be.

One could argue that this was nothing more than the imaginative musings of an overly cocky teenager intent on making it as a rock star, but the truth is, we did that radio appearance and it went well. We were very kind to the people there and took photos with everyone in the office who asked for one. Even if some of them were grabbing pictures just to laugh at us later, the important thing was they paid attention.

A few days later, our radio programming person asked me, "What happened at WEBN in Cincinnati?" I told him I thought we were well received. "They said that you guys were just boring on the air. You wouldn't talk to anybody. You were so to yourselves. You were rude." This feedback served only to convince me I must've been right all along.

It reinforced my long-internalized belief that I couldn't do *anything* without someone dismissing me in response. Okay, so I'm too polite for you or too mild-mannered? People will form opinions about me no matter how pleasant I am in conversation. So, I figured, "Why not go further into the persona? Give them what they expected in the first place."

Attitude propelled us as we stayed on the road through the end of 2010 with the Entertainment or Death and the Pins and Needles tours.

It became a self-fulfilling prophecy. This whole notion that we were these outcasts, freaks who championed the downtrodden and cast aside, we embraced it, full stop.

We looked the part, which helped to keep us immersed in this world of adversarial combat. We couldn't step into a restaurant without being the weirdest-looking people there, and that became an increasingly comfortable place for us to be. After all, how can I get on stage and proclaim my solidarity with the outcasts if I'm not an outcast myself? Short of purposefully contracting leprosy, how much more could I stand apart?

We were such road dogs, did so much press, and took every promotional opportunity we could manage. *Set the World On Fire* was our first major-label album, which meant it had a lot of extra push behind it. We felt like we had to do everything that came our way, every signing offered, and every radio station visit, whatever it was.

And we had to continue to up the ante with our personas, to be more outrageous, make more of an impression, to give even more of ourselves onstage, in every performance.

It was that attitude that led me to do something stupid on stage, an overly ambitious climb and subsequent fall, which sent me to the hospital with three broken ribs.

20

HOLLYWOOD & HIGHLAND

THE NEIGHBORHOOD NEAR THE intersection of Hollywood Boulevard and Highland Avenue is home to famous landmark theaters like Grauman's Chinese, where the first *Star Wars* premiered, and the Kodak, home to the Oscars. The Musician's Institute, filled with rock 'n' roll hopefuls from around the country, is nearby. Jimmy Kimmel tapes his television show across the street from the Hollywood & Highland Center. On any given day, actors dressed as characters like Spider-Man, Batman, Marilyn Monroe, and Captain Jack Sparrow wander around, bumping into aspiring rappers asking a passerby to listen to a mixtape. I suppose it made sense that would be the place where I snapped my ribcage.

We took a break during the making of *Set the World on Fire* to do the God Save the Scream Tour in the UK and the AP Tour. The day the album dropped, June 14, the title track appeared on the *Transformers: Dark of the Moon* soundtrack, alongside My Chemical Romance, Linkin Park, and Paramore, among other high-profile artists. A major label, headlining tours, landing on soundtracks with more prominent bands—I was living my dream.

I was also throwing myself more intensely into each performance, pouring every ounce of energy I could muster into being this semi-villainous antagonistic character with the same reckless dedication I put into pouring booze into my body. We were already enduring the exhaustive schedule of shows, signings, interviews, and traveling that comes with any developing band's new record, but I just continued to push harder.

We spent the Saturday of release week meeting fans at various Hot Topic locations around Southern California. Our first stop was in Ontario, which is about forty miles from Los Angeles. Next, we arrived at a Hot Topic in a West Covina shopping plaza. Our last stop was at the Hollywood & Highland shopping center location. The Virgin Megastore, The Hard Rock Café, a Rolling Stone store, music was everywhere. (For a short time, the *TRL* style syndicated show *On Air with Ryan Seacrest* broadcast live from there.)

We'd worn our warpaint all day long. Remember, this wasn't stage makeup. It was acrylic paint, the kind available at local craft stores. It didn't allow our pores to breathe because it's not intended for human skin. By about six in the evening, after wearing it all day, we just felt heavy. The paint hardened and tightened, making us feel claustrophobic.

The most effective method we'd devised to deal with the discomfort delivered by a day's worth of warpaint was the same solution we had for everything else: we got drunk. That day at Hollywood & Highland was no different. We finished out the last signing and spent the next few hours downing shots, cocktails, and beer, until our ten p.m. performance.

I can't overstate how important it was to me to do something unforgettable. I continuously challenged myself to exceed my expectations in terms of showmanship, with every appearance. "What can I do that is going to be spectacular? What will cement this moment in everyone's memory as something provocative and grand?"

I'd just turned twenty a few months before. I remained so uncomfortable in my skin, so driven by "revenge" and the isolation I'd felt since childhood, that it was easy to be swept away in this fantastical alter ego I presented to the world. Alice Cooper has spoken about leaving the character of "Alice" on the stage. I hadn't learned that lesson.

I wouldn't just show up and play the songs. I had to drive people nuts. We needed to elicit some kind of passion from the crowd, whether it was positive or negative.

I could endure the hatred. I'd handle the heckling, the gossip, the "slings and arrows" of spite on social media. What I wouldn't abide was to be ignored. My childhood insistence to be seen, heard, and understood (even if that meant rejection) never wavered.

As the hour drew closer to our performance at Hollywood & Highland, I became supremely focused on the opportunity to imprint Black Veil Brides on the psyche of the world at large, given that we were setting foot on what I saw as a "world stage." It was a heavily trafficked tourist area. To put it in football terms, as the alcohol soaked my brain, I resolved to make some sort of "splash play." The moments replayed on ESPN.

Set the World on Fire? I wanted to melt the statues of the stars at nearby Madame Tussaud's Wax Museum. (Metaphorically speaking, of course. I don't condone arson.)

Usually, I'd become so exhausted from going completely crazy onstage that I wouldn't have enough breath left to finish the songs the fans wanted to hear by the end of the night. The alcohol started to wear off, and my mind and body would simply crash.

I'd all but kill myself during the first few songs in those days, running back and forth, falling, jumping off of speakers. As we started playing at Hollywood & Highland, I surveyed my surroundings and discovered these weird giant statues of elephants. Immediately, I wanted to climb up to those elephants and then leap back onto the stage.

There was no real route to the top of those statues. In my inebriated, adrenaline-fueled state, the fact that the logistics of my plan were all but impossible didn't matter to me. Plus, I was wearing cowboy boots with zero traction. Those steps were marble.

It was "beginning-of-the-show, amped-up Andy." About halfway through the first song, I simply couldn't contain my excitement any longer. I hopped off the stage and started climbing up to the first platform. Straight away, I nearly slipped. "Whoa, this isn't good."

But I powered upward. I took a giant step up to the second platform, followed by an even bigger stride toward the third. As I awkwardly worked to establish some kind of solid footing on there, I realized that there's no way I would be able to reach the very top.

I had zero awareness of anything else that was happening, completely immersed in my little world. I wasn't a total fool; even in my drunken stupor, I knew I'd reached my limit and should not attempt to get any farther up. I figured I'd climbed far enough, anyway. It would still look pretty badass and crazy to jump from that height, right?

I started to lose my balance. I sat down. I wasn't very strong, but the alcohol told me otherwise. I believed I could use my arms to catapult myself down and that I'd land feet first on the stage. My body was basically in the shape of a capital letter "L" on its side. In my mind, I should've been able to push the "L" onto the stage and simply go end over end, facing safely up. Instead, when I pushed off, I just fell straight down.

In my descent, I smashed into the other pillars below. The ninth, tenth, and eleventh ribs on the left side of my body were all broken. My eleventh rib shattered into basic shrapnel. It was just obliterated. By the time I hit the ground, I could barely breathe.

There wasn't any professional medical staff on hand, but a security guard saw what happened and rushed over to my side. He must've taken a CPR class at some point. I'd broken the ribs on the left side of my body, had the wind knocked out of me, and I was in almost unimaginable pain. The security guard turned me over onto my back and started CPR. Yes, this large, strong gentleman gave me chest compressions.

I'll never forget what I heard as he pushed down on my sternum. It sounded like boots stomping all over bubble wrap. I couldn't speak. I tried to force some kind of noise out of my throat so he'd know I was conscious and that he should quit. Eventually, I was lifted back onto my feet and somehow, improbably, finished the show. Or so I was told.

I didn't know where I was afterward. I have no memory of the remaining set, as I must have been in a state of shock. I don't recall being on stage after my fall. A large column obstructed the rest of the band's view to where I was before the fall, so I was never in their line of sight when it happened. All they knew was that I'd left the stage for a while.

It's bizarre for me to watch videos of it. I was calling out songs that indeed weren't on the setlist because they were songs we'd never done live. In retrospect, it's pretty hilarious that my subconscious went searching for deep cuts. One would think my autopilot would default to the most prominent songs we always played. But no, my subconscious mind was like, "This could be the last show I ever do. Let's break out the B-sides!"

The next thing I remember was the security guard wrapping me up in this big rubber tire type thing. The best way I can describe it? It was like something a person might cover a beam in a two-car garage with so there'd be something soft if a car door opened into it.

I heard someone wonder aloud whether they should call an ambulance. Another person said no. I had my cell phone, so I started texting a few people, like my parents and our tour manager. I wanted to let them know I was headed to the hospital and that my phone would probably be off for a while. I'm glad I had the presence of mind to at least let these important people know that something was up.

Our TM, Jon, had his problems to deal with back at Hollywood & Highland. He's since told me there was chaos in the immediate aftermath of our performance. It was a shopping center, not a concert venue, so there were no professional stagehands. It was just a few mall employees working as show staff for the day. They didn't know what belonged to whom, so people tried to steal our gear. In those days, most of our fans came dressed like us, in full makeup. It looked like band members grabbing equipment.

A guy dressed precisely like Jinxx, from head to toe, picked up a guitar case (which was empty) and walked off with it. Jon chased him down and grabbed it back.

Pulling into the hospital parking lot, we saw giant statues of building blocks (the letter "A" and the letter "B") and a giant cuddly cartoon bear. The entryway was super colorful. I thought to myself, "I feel like this might be a children's hospital..."

The pain was still excruciating, despite the fact I was still very drunk. I cursed like a sailor as we walked inside, my face smeared with red lipstick, my body covered in black paint. My pants were two-tone leopard print spandex with the rubber tire type thing the security guard wrapped around me. The poor kids who were patients at the hospital must've thought I'd just crawled out of the grave and into their waking nightmares.

Everyone else realized our mistake, so we got back in the car and headed across the street to the *grownup* hospital, a Kaiser Permanente location on Sunset Boulevard. The medical staff insisted on running blood tests before they would admit me into a room.

I kept repeating to them: "I'm not on drugs! I'm *drunk*. But I'm not on drugs!"

Because of the hardened paint all over me, they couldn't find a vein in which to stick a needle. The nurses stabbed at me repeatedly as they tried to draw blood. (I have a tiny scar.)

"I leaped thirty feet and broke my ribs." Did you fall thirty feet? "No. I *leaped* 30 feet."

Next, they tried to get an IV into me to feed me painkillers so I'd stop screaming. They tried getting the paint off with alcohol on a swab, but it just didn't work. Because it's acrylic craft store paint, they had to scrape it off. Like, intensely scrape away at it.

I finally explained to them that I was a "theatrical performer," which seemed to relax them about how I looked and what had happened, like a stage mishap during a play.

My mom got on a plane and arrived the next day. My ex and I had broken up several weeks before, but she showed up to support me as well. I hadn't seen my cousin Joe in about two years before he came to see me in the hospital.

(He'd moved to Los Angeles the same week I broke my ribs, and we were both eager to reconnect.)

After my discharge, I went to stay in a hotel room in West Hollywood, a few blocks down the road from the world-famous Whisky A Go Go on Sunset Boulevard.

It was during release week for our first major-label album and about a week before we were scheduled to leave for the summer on Warped Tour. We missed the first week of the tour as I was laid up in the hotel room, recovering from the accident for about ten days. I saw the first sales figures for *Set the World On Fire* as I had enemas administered so I could pass some of the excess cartilage lodged in my system.

I walked by a mirror in the hotel room one morning and realized I could very well look pregnant by the time I hit the stage at Warped Tour. I had to eat, but it was too painful to poop, so my stomach was all distended. All I could do was lie around and try to heal.

Matt Good stayed with me for the entire time I was in the hotel room. Richard Villa brought over a copy of Ridley Scott's 1985 romantic fantasy classic *Legend* on DVD. I had so few things to entertain myself with that I ended up watching *Legend* repeatedly.

Tim Curry from *The Rocky Horror Picture Show* plays Darkness, a big devil creature that wants to create endless night by eliminating the last of the unicorns. Mia Sara from *Ferris Bueller's Day Off* (and Jean Claude Van Damme's *Timecop*) plays the damsel in distress, and Tom Cruise is the hero, Jack O' The Green. I consumed every single special feature on the disc and all of the director's commentary.

It was Ridley Scott's follow-up to *Blade Runner*. I learned all about how Oingo Boingo, the group best known for "Dead Man's Party" (as heard in the late Rodney Dangerfield's *Back to School*) and "Weird Science" (from the classic comedy of the same name), was supposed to be involved with *Legend* but it didn't work out. Scott continuously apologizes for Oingo Boingo's absence from the finished film. (Incidentally, Oingo Boingo's front man, Danny Elfman, became a legendary film composer.)

At a certain point, I couldn't handle another frame of *Legend*, so I started channel surfing. I landed on NBC and discovered this *American Idol*-style singing competition, *The Voice*. These were reruns, so I was able to watch almost the entire first season in a single day. (The runner-up on that inaugural season was Dia Frampton of Meg & Dia.)

When I was finally able to drag myself onto the tour bus, I was excited to see what Warped Tour had in store. The crowds didn't quite know what to expect from us.

Various rumors surrounded the band. We'd cultivated a certain mystique that was polarizing. I could almost feel the apprehension, nervous anticipation, and overall confusion in the air that surrounded us. Despite the harrowing injury at Hollywood & Highland, I remained determined to push the envelope and up the ante.

We kicked against the limits of what we were "allowed" to do. We were fortunate that Warped Tour founder Kevin Lyman didn't kick us off of the trek immediately.

We decided at one point that we'd like to get into the Guinness Book of World Records by smashing more guitars than any other band. We'd usually end up breaking the *stage*.

Part of the joy of Warped is the discovery of new and different things. I had no problem politely watching bands I wasn't interested in while waiting for the groups I came to see. It never occurred to me to wantonly telegraph aggression toward the people onstage.

Warped Tour was the setting for many important moments in my life, from my developmental years in Cincinnati to all of the jaunts with Black Veil Brides and touring as Andy Black. But all of these crucial experiences pale in comparison to the most significant of them all: Vans Warped Tour is where I met my wife, Juliet Nicole Simms.

Juliet was born in San Francisco, earning her musician stripes as singer and guitarist for the band Automatic Loveletter, formed in Tampa, Florida. Her brother Tommy was briefly in the band at one point. The group paid their dues on the road and in the studio. Fuse TV personality Alison Hagendorf helped them secure a deal with Epic/ Sony, who put them in the studio with producer Matt Squire (Panic! At The Disco, All Time Low).

She's amazing. Super talented, driven, courageous, smart, charming, and beautiful.

Juliet snuck onto the Warped Tour in 2008 armed with nothing more than her acoustic guitar and her voice. Kevin was so impressed with her that he eventually offered her official slots on the tour. We met on Warped in 2011.

Her voice and beauty struck me before we'd spoken a single word to each other. Her lyrics struck a chord with me as well; I heard a kindred spirit in her songs. My big romantic idea was to go and watch her set every day and just stand awkwardly watching till she noticed me. (This was a terrible plan, and I do not recommend copying it.)

Thankfully she came to watch Black Veil Brides, too. Once we started talking, the attraction was mutual, and our feelings for one another developed rapidly.

I asked her to move to Los Angeles immediately after we started dating. I was all in.

I was twenty years old and completely smitten with the woman who would become my wife. I just thought, "No matter what, this is what I want. She is what's important to me."

I counted down the days until we could be together in California.

I desperately wanted to get myself into a real apartment before she arrived. I didn't know Juliet had already been to the Compound. I just knew I didn't want her to see me living there. It was no longer a representation of me. Though I was still drinking every day, I wanted to show her a better version of myself, maybe someone closer to who I'd always been inside. I didn't want her to live with this "character" I cultivated.

Matt Good and I were still interested in being roommates. When Juliet and I arrived in Los Angeles, I put us in a Motel 8 until we were able to find a place. I went by the Compound to get what little things I had while Jake was still living there. Matt lived with Juliet and me until he met the girl that would become *his* wife and moved to Arizona.

Kevin Lyman took Juliet under his wing, so when she and I started dating, I became closer to him as well. We went to his house for dinner often, enjoying our time with him, his wife, and their children. He's someone who will always offer honest answers to my questions, and he has so much experience in the touring business.

The Compound continued to be something of a party place for a time, but it never recaptured its original "glory." Eventually, Jake managed to turn it into a respectable bachelor pad for himself. He painted the walls and put a few nicer things around. (It's funny to think someone is living there now with no idea of the things that once went on.)

I was still driving my '98 Cadillac the first time I met Juliet's father. He came to visit us. He'd taken a taxi to the restaurant where we had dinner, and for some reason, I thought it'd be a good idea to offer him a ride back to where he was staying. After this came out of my mouth, I remembered that my car was full of Junior Mints, empty cans, clothing, and probably more than one bottle of urine. I spent five minutes in the parking garage cleaning out all of this garbage and putting it in the trunk right in front of him.

That was my first experience with my future father-in-law.

Later that year, my new girlfriend was asked to audition for *The Voice* and didn't know anything about it. I was in this uniquely informed position to explain everything about it because I'd watched an entire season from a hotel bed. (It would turn out to be the only time I'd ever know anything about a reality TV series she hadn't seen herself.)

I was very happy with Juliet and, somewhere inside, started to feel a tug back toward my center. I knew this adversarial villain wasn't me; I should begin to rein it in.

Unfortunately, the self-inflicted injury spree I started at Hollywood & Highland wasn't over.

The day of Juliet's first blind audition for *The Voice*, I was in Europe breaking my face.

It was late October 2011 at a show in Luxembourg. I fractured my skull and broke my nose straight down the center. It was a giant theater we couldn't possibly have filled. We weren't drawing huge crowds on the mainland as it was, but by our estimation, it would have taken the entire population of this town to pack *that* place. It's hard enough to be in the spirited romantic throes of a blossoming relationship and immediately have to tear away from each other to travel overseas for several weeks. It was an insult to injury (no pun intended) to have to get on stage and play this cavernous empty theater.

These were the days of terrible international phone service. I called Juliet from Luxembourg. It was hard to communicate over a shaky connection when I would have rather been at her side. As per usual, in those days, I drowned my emotions in alcohol.

By the time we went on stage, I was wasted, pulling my usual onstage antics. I writhed, crawled, stomped, sprinted back and forth. Toward the end of our set, I rolled underneath the drum riser. I hadn't noticed the pole that went through the back of the riser, so when I tried to get back on my feet, I smashed my face with a loud crack.

Robert Murphy, a longtime crewmember who is now a pretty successful tattoo artist, saw what happened. I walked up to him and asked, "Is my nose broken?" He said, "Nah."

I turned around and started singing again. That's when the pain struck me. I swiveled in the opposite direction and looked at Jonathan, whose eyes were as wide as pizzas. I pointed to my nose and made a quizzical face. His jaw dropped.

I rushed off stage. Jon and I studied my face in a backstage mirror, trying to determine what exactly was happening to it. It looked like my nose was broken, but the pain was actually in my *skull*. We weren't sure how to handle that. I mean, we aren't doctors.

We had to cancel a bunch of tour dates, so I posted photos of my face online so people would know the injuries were severe enough to postpone the gigs. We hate canceling shows. Often when a band has to cancel something, the press and fans won't give them the benefit of the doubt, but our fans are much more forgiving. Nevertheless, we wanted to get something out there. Then it was off to London to plot our next move.

In England, we played one show as a test to see whether I could make it through the rest of the European gigs. My face blew up like a balloon. We had a short US headlining tour scheduled for November of that year, followed by a lengthy arena run with Avenged Sevenfold, Hollywood Undead, and Asking Alexandria, also in America.

I became preoccupied with *that* injury, which meant the fact that I'd broken my ribs just a few months before went on the backburner. I was more or less self-medicating with alcohol, so as time went on, as a young adult partying all of the time, the last thing I'd think when I had some sort of random pain in my sides was "I should get that checked."

Physical therapy? I didn't have health insurance, and I didn't have the kind of money to go out of pocket, either. I was still trying to figure out how to pay the initial hospital bills. I needed money to stay out of the Compound and maintain my new home with Juliet.

We had a very modest one-bedroom apartment, but it still required a sizeable portion of our income every month. It was also Los Angeles. My share of the rent at the Compound had been $500 per month, and that was living with three other people.

When deciding between whether I'd spend money on doctors to make sure my ribs healed properly or purchasing something for the apartment, I always chose the latter. It may have been a cheap piece from Ikea, but it was furniture. I picked groceries over physical therapy. I suspected my insides were out of whack, but I ignored it.

I could've asked my parents for help. We've always been so close, but I was at an age where I wasn't telling them everything. I didn't want to worry them with every ache and pain or burden them with financial obligation. I wanted them to think everything was fine.

I should have told them I needed to have some tests done. As I mentioned earlier in the book, my parents are my best friends. They were my heroes. Getting drunk and jumping off of things was my fault, my problem, in service of acting like this outcast villain.

21

HEROES & VILLAINS

MY MOM AND DAD were my first heroes. Gene Simmons, Paul Stanley, and Matt Skiba entered my hall of fame next. My parents made it possible for me to create Black Veil Brides, and Black Veil Brides paved the way for my eventual encounters with the artists whose music and imagery meant so much to me growing up.

We closed out 2011 with an EP that paid tribute to some of those heroes. *Rebels* included "Coffin," an unreleased track from the *Set the World on Fire* recording session, a six-minute director's cut of the "Rebel Love Song" music video, and two cover songs. We chose Billy Idol's eighties anthem "Rebel Yell" and "Unholy" by KISS, which was one of the songs cowritten for *Revenge* with ex-guitarist Vinnie

Vincent, who played on *Creatures of the Night* (though Ace was on the album's cover) and officially as part of *Lick it Up*.

"Coffin" continues to be my favorite from that era and one of my favorites of our songs overall. When I wrote that song, I was thinking a lot about where I lived, which for about a year was essentially inside a "coffin," rolling around on the road everywhere. It's also about people telling us that the band was just a fad and that we still needed "that" song. A lot of older groups said to us, "Oh, you guys would be huge if you just had *that* song." The spirit of "Coffin" is one of defiance. Nobody is going to take this dream away.

Around the time we released our second album and follow-up EP, there were outside voices that insisted things were going to happen for us commercially, though they ultimately did not. As much as we worked to keep our expectations reasonable internally, it was difficult to bounce back from what we were led to believe *might* happen for us.

As we finished up the touring cycle for *Set the World on Fire*, I'd grown a bit unhappy with the direction the band had taken. With each new success, the perception of the group and the related expectations were just not congruent with how I saw it or who I wanted to be.

The hair metal Sunset Strip era vibe, the over-sexualization of everything—those were not things I grew up loving or inspired by, yet they were getting pushed to the forefront. Look, I'm not going to say I wasn't doing the whole "tease your hair up and dress like the Crüe" thing. We were all there, and we were all doing it. But the early Crüe image to me was more of a bridge from KISS and the darker horror punk stuff I loved, like the Misfits. I was never even into the Mötley Crüe discography. I've said this in interviews over the years. I knew the hits, but I wasn't introduced to the deeper cuts till later in life.

I was never interested in writing songs about partying or getting laid. The expectation surrounding us was that the band would go further in that direction, so I found myself playing into it, as far as the things I'd say in interviews or agree to—this whole "sleazy" eighties glam thing. And by the end of the touring for *Set the World on Fire*, I'd just had enough. I knew we were no longer sending the message I'd wanted for the band on *We Stitch These Wounds*. I had zero interest in the whole eighties hair metal thing for us.

I mean, I was happy that the band was becoming much more successful. The momentum was significant. But change was necessary. I sat on an airplane on the way home from tour and started sketching out some ideas for the next phase of the band. I wrote what became the basis for the whole story of *Wretched and Divine* during a single flight, all on the "Notes" section of my iPhone. After we landed, I sent it over to everyone on our team.

Pat Fogarty, Richard Villa, and I further developed the ideas thematically and visually. We worked on a "bible" for the story—a bible, in this case, is a reference guide a writer or team will put together with information on characters, design elements, sets, and principal components of a television series, film franchise, comic book series, or other media.

We'd decided we'd make our next album with producer Sean Beavan, a fellow Ohio native. He had mixed vital records by Nine Inch Nails and produced Marilyn Manson's big breakout albums, *Antichrist Superstar* and *Mechanical Animals*. As I mentioned, we'd been fortunate enough to have the title track from *Set the World on Fire* secure a place on the soundtrack for *Transformers: Dark of the Moon,* and we were even more ecstatic about the chance to have a song on the soundtrack for Marvel's *The Avengers*.

There was only a very brief period between the end of the previous tour and working with Sean. We made the *Avengers* song "Unbroken" and had a great time working with him, so we began to move forward into the next album, tracking drums for demos of songs that were *Set the World on Fire*-esque in terms of feel. Around this time, I learned that A-list producer John Feldmann was interested in writing some songs with me.

Feldmann is the front person for Goldfinger, but at this point is best known for having his fingerprints on some thirty-five million albums sold around the world, including big records from The Used and Panic! at the Disco, and later, 5 Seconds of Summer and Blink-182. He invited me to his house just to kick around some ideas, but once I started explaining the concept behind what I wanted to do, he became fascinated by the plans. "Your album needs to be operatic in scale," he told me. "Lots of instrumentation, moods, and sounds."

Everything he suggested ran counter to what was happening in the studio with Sean, which was fine, but it felt like *Set the World On Fire Part II*. I worked a bit with John, then returned with Jake and Jinxx. Together, we wrote "We

Don't Belong." When we got the demo back for "We Don't Belong," it sounded exactly how I'd envisioned *Wretched and Divine* should. "This is the sound of the story I want to tell," I thought.

The instrumentation, the cinematic Danny Elfman–style flair, the huge chorus that's heavy but melodic—it was all perfect to me. Perhaps most importantly, it didn't at all sound like an eighties hair metal Sunset Strip band. It was so much more ambitious and grandiose.

Unfortunately, I found myself with the unenviable task, at twenty years old, of walking into a studio and telling a big producer I very much liked and respected that we were cutting him loose. I should add that at that point, we hadn't even made a deal with Feldmann. For all I knew, he wouldn't be available or affordable to us when we asked him to do it. All I knew for sure was that the stuff we were doing with Sean wasn't what we needed.

I went to the studio and asked Sean to step outside with me. I tried to talk it through as diplomatically as possible. It led to a very awkward situation where Sean went back inside and told CC to tear down his drums. "I was just fired, so we're done tracking." (Sean is a wonderful person whom I was fortunate enough to run into in subsequent years.)

Almost immediately, I was on the phone with Feldmann, or "Feldy" as his friends call him. "Hey, I just fired our producer. So, um, do you think you might want to make our record?"

We were already behind schedule, and now we'd be setting things back even further by starting over. We'd also spent a significant portion of the budget; there was no reason to demand Sean return any deposits. He'd done nothing "wrong" and was entitled to whatever we'd agreed then. Feldy was making something else at the moment but was very much interested and assured me we could work something out.

We must have missed three separate release dates with that album. But it was worth it. Feldy understood what I wanted to do. He believed in the concept. We didn't have the time or resources necessary to pull it off, but we pulled it off anyway. Once the label was able to hear what we made with Feldmann, they understood the decision.

Our product manager became enough of a believer that he was able to get Universal to open the checkbook for the album's promotion, including the making of the counterpart film. Even though we'd yet to land a single radio hit for them, they got behind the idea. They gave us enough to go out to the El Mirage Dry Lake Bed in the Mojave Desert to execute the visual side of *Wretched and Divine* precisely the way I wanted to do it.

I was twenty years old with a little bit of success and the power to make the kind of concept album I'd always wanted to make. My cousin Joe shot footage of us every day in the studio. When I watched the footage back a few years later, I would cringe a bit, seeing my lack of tact in dealing with other people at times. There's a scene in the documentary where Jinxx said he thought perhaps the chorus to "Devil's Choir" was a little too poppy for us. And I said something like, "Yeah, don't you hate it when a song is good and people like it?" I acted like a dick. I was just not nice. But I was a horse with blinders on, because I had absolute confidence in my vision for the album. Most of the guys wanted to make *Set the World on Fire* again, or even a more aggressive traditional heavy metal album.

I wanted a Black Veil Brides rock opera. Between the push and pull of what they wanted and what I wanted, I think we got something somewhere between the two, which is why the record works as well as it does. The album gave us our first RIAA gold-certified single.

It was going to be the big single, and yet it was a happy accident how it came about. The day we wrote "In the End," we'd spent several hours working on a *different* song, which we ultimately scrapped. By the early evening, we knew it wasn't working. So, we decided to start completely over with a different idea, and that became "In the End."

We released "In the End" on Halloween in 2012. The album followed in January 2013. *Wretched and Divine: The Story of the Wild Ones* became the No. 2 Hard Rock Album in America when it debuted. It went to No. 5 on Billboard's Top Album Sales chart and No. 7 on the Billboard 200. The success of the album helped us welcome a renewed optimism.

We started playing bigger venues. We spent 2013 on The Church of the Wild Ones Tour, the *Kerrang!* Tour; the Wild Ones tour; another Vans Warped Tour; and the Monster Energy Outbreak tour, during which we often covered "Fiend Club" by the Misfits.

The Misfits, at that point "resurrected" and fronted by bassist Jerry Only, owed much of their notoriety to Metallica, who had covered several of their songs. Metallica, of course, is the biggest heavy metal band in the world. Their self-titled fifth album, colloquially referred to as *The Black Album* due to its stark cover, became the biggest album of the Soundscan era—that is to say, the biggest album released since 1991 when Nielsen began counting album sales with the universally recognized Soundscan calculation.

The Black Album was a turning point for both Metallica and heavy metal culture. The thrash metal innovators took a risk hiring producer Bob Rock, who had made successful albums with Bon Jovi and the Crüe, two bands very much in aesthetic opposition to what Metallica was doing. (In fact, James Hetfield owned a guitar with "Kill Bon Jovi" written on it and in the documentary about the making of the album, the band throws darts at posters of hair metal guys.) It came out a few months before my first birthday, and like so many things from before my time, I was aware of the sea change it had caused in rock.

Several heavy bands who emerged from the under-ground have chased the *Black Album* idea since then—a mas-sive-sounding album, more stripped-down songs, self-titled, even. When we learned that Bob Rock himself had heard our band and wanted to meet us, we were thrilled. And coming off the high concept grandiosity of album three, it felt like it was time for our own *Black Album* moment. Plus, like Feldy, Bob was also a musician himself.

Blasko arranged a lunch with Bob and the band at Swingers Diner, a relatively "hip" twenty-four-hour eatery on Beverly Boulevard. in Los Angeles. I had never met

Bob, but seeing him in person was surreal given that I was so familiar with him and his work. We'd seen him in the Metallica documentaries, so when he sat down at Swingers, we instantly recognized his blond hair, black leather jacket, and Saint Laurent boots.

As we introduced ourselves to each other, as if my brain needed this extra overload, Matt Skiba of Alkaline Trio sat down in the chair right behind Bob. He was at Swingers, too, but by himself, reading a newspaper. He noticed Bob and become interested in what was happening. I'm sure there were essential career things discussed between the band, our manager, and this A-list producer, but my focus turned solely on Skiba.

I avoided meeting him for years. We had mutual friends. Once, a buddy called me in the middle of the night to tell me he'd been drinking with Skiba and that I should come to hang out. No thanks! I hadn't been drinking that night, so I'd be starting from zero while they were already at about seventy. How much more suspicious could I seem than if I were to show up sober and just try to "hang out" with him? I have multiple visible Alkaline Trio tattoos. There was no way I could have shown up without seeming like an interloper.

I put the guy on a pedestal, and I wanted to keep him there. But as I walked to my car after the Bob Rock meeting, I realized, "This may be my best chance just to tell him something simple about how much his music has meant to me." He was alone, so I wouldn't be interrupting a conversation. He had seen our meeting and looked curious about it. I planned to walk back and say, "Hey, big fan, your music means a lot to me, I just wanted to say that," then leave. (I wasn't going to mention that I was also in a band.)

I know I appreciate it when people approach me to say something nice and don't try to "Bogart" my day. I figured he probably recognized Bob and knew I'd been with him, so he needn't fear I was an overzealous lunatic wandering in from the street to attack him.

But then my lizard brain told me, "Say something *else!*" An alarm sounded in my head, reminding me that Black Veil Brides and Alkaline Trio would be on the Soundwave tour in Australia together. So, at the moment, I figured if I told him I'd see him soon on tour, it would communicate that I was also in a band without directly saying it and coming off like a braggart. Unfortunately, how it all came out at the moment was like this:

"Hey, Matt! My name is Andy. I'm a huge fan. Your music influenced me a lot, and I just wanted to let you know that I will see you in Australia." And then I left.

I was about halfway to my car when I realized I must've sounded like a complete crazy person. No matter, I reassured myself. "I know how Soundwave works. It will all be fine because we'll probably have a flight together or run into each other in a hotel lobby," as the bands travel together, and we tended to end up seeing everyone.

Soundwave was only a week away. The whole awkward story could be put to bed right there. How could it get any worse, right?

We spent our first night in Sydney at the hotel bar. I stepped outside for a cigarette. To exit to the smoking area, I had to navigate a narrow passageway crowded with band and crew guys in town for Soundwave, girls there to meet groups, locals, and staff.

As I slowly squeezed through the crowd, I spotted, to my immediate left, Matt Skiba. As I went past him, a girl swiveled in her chair and smacked his ass. I watched like it was in slow motion. He and I made eye contact. It was clear he thought *I* had hit his ass.

I ran outside. Could this get any worse? I mean, he could've been forgiven for thinking that I'd "followed" him to Australia and then sexually assaulted him. The following night, I had no intention of going out again. I got a call that evening from Jeremiah Scott, who toured with us as our front of house engineer for many years. Jeremiah is an easygoing and charismatic guy who is not concerned with Alkaline Trio one way or another. He listens to Amon Amarth. And he looks like he could be *in* Amon Amarth, more or less.

"I've been at the bar all night hanging out with that guy from that band you like," he told me with his distinctive Southern gentleman charm. "The guy Matt. Matt...something."

"I mentioned who I'm here working with, and he told me loves the *Wretched and Divine* album," he continued. "Do you want to come down to the bar and meet him?"

At first I said no. But Jeremiah was earnest and made a strong case to get me to come down and say hello to one of my heroes. I think, "Okay, this time there's no way there's anything that can go wrong. He's been hanging out with Jeremiah all night. Jeremiah will be my social awkwardness buffer."

I went down, and Jeremiah introduced the two of us. As I shook Skiba's hand, it was like the clouds parted for a moment, and everything was finally okay. He said, "Hey, man, it's so crazy, I didn't realize who you were. I didn't recognize you. But I'm a fan of what you guys do. It's nice to meet you." I was like, "Yeah, I'm so sorry that everything has been so strange so far." And he's like, "Yeah, we've had a kind of wild time, huh?"

Just as he was casually acknowledging how awkward things had been till that point, in a way that put me at ease, this guy who had been standing right next to Matt started losing his mind. "No! No! No!" He roared. "Matt! I *hate* this Andy guy!"

It turned out Matt's friend was in Street Dogs! I had recounted that story about meeting his singer in an interview, and apparently, they weren't happy about it. This guy held a bit of a grudge and wanted me to know it.

Luckily the Street Dogs guy was cool, and after talking for a bit, we parted on good terms. But Skiba had quietly slipped away when the conversation started. Man, it didn't seem like I could meet this particular hero without something awkward happening.

The first time I ran into Gene was even *more* awkward than meeting Matt.

We all met Gene Simmons at the NAMM Show, the trade-only event for the musical gear industry, which happens in January each year at the Anaheim Convention Center, near Disneyland, in Orange County, California. It was 2009, and BVB had descended on the convention floor looking very much like, you know, Black Veil Brides in 2009.

Simmons was there with a camera crew from his A&E reality TV series. *Gene Simmons Family Jewels* followed Gene and his longtime partner/wife, former *Playboy* model Shannon Tweed, and their two kids, as they navigated domestic life. (Remember what I said about KISS paying attention to pop culture trends with acute business savvy? *Family Jewels* started airing about a year after *The Osbournes* went off the air.)

Given what we looked like, it was a no-brainer for his television producers to approach us and ask to grab a moment with Gene for the show. Honestly, I didn't like it. I wasn't thrilled to be used as a silly novelty, one influenced by KISS, for reality television.

Perhaps I was still taking a page out of his book when I burst out with some kind of big bravado and told him something like, "We're Black Veil Brides and we're going to take over" or "we're going to be bigger than you." It was snarky, but I certainly wasn't serious.

He laughed. But then I got mad about the *way* he laughed. Something about his cackle seemed to communicate that he wasn't in on the joke. He didn't understand the "wink."

Of course, I wasn't sincerely suggesting to the guy from KISS that my band was going to be bigger than his. I was just trying to show that we had balls too and that we were not some throwaway joke or wannabes to exploit for a dumb little TV bit.

You will know who I am. That's what I was trying to say. The whole interaction left a bad taste in my mouth, which led directly to me acting like a crazy person when we played the *Golden Gods* in 2012, the year Alice Cooper gave us that excellent introduction.

Gene and his family were the only people in the upper deck of the theater when we went on. Naturally, I was very drunk. When I saw Gene, something inside of me said, "Remember how he laughed at you and you didn't like it? This is your moment.

"You should act like a lunatic. Right now."

I humped the ground, beat the hell out of myself, and turned it into the most unhinged Iggy Pop style performance of my career. My voice sounded awful because I didn't focus on how I was singing whatsoever. The singular purpose that drove my performance that night was to make Gene Simmons of KISS uncomfortable. He was up there looking down at us (literally!), and I wanted to get my band inside of his head.

As always, as it had been throughout my life, I wouldn't stand for being dismissed.

There's no way he could have kept avoiding us, anyway. Gene and I were both depicted on the illustrated cover of *Revolver's 100 Greatest Living Rock Stars* issue in a beautiful image rendered by artist Jason Edmiston. Gene posted that cover on his social media. I wanted him to know I wasn't nuts back at NAMM 2009 when I insisted that my band was going to matter someday, that we would be meaningful, significant.

At some point, we were offered some shows with KISS, but the money was too low to make sense for us and, more importantly, there wasn't much to be gained by opening for them. That crowd cares only about the headliner, and I know that from experience. I went to dozens of KISS shows and never cared about the openers. From First to Last played with KISS, and my understanding from Matt Good was that on several nights there were even small kids, upon their dads' shoulders, flipping off the opening band.

My encounter with Paul Stanley, Gene's longtime comrade-at-arms, went much better, and like Matt Skiba, it was thanks to Bob Rock, albeit in an even more direct way.

I read Stanley's memoir, *Face the Music: A Life Exposed*, shortly after its 2014 release. As I finished it, I thought about how much I liked it and how it'd be nice to tell him so if I ever had the opportunity. Then literally the same week, I went to the first preproduction session for the album we made with Bob Rock, titled simply *Black Veil Brides*, and Paul Stanley was rehearsing in the room right next door to ours. (He was running through songs with his R&B revue, Soul Station, who play intimate club shows.)

For a moment, I thought perhaps I had "manifested" that situation by thinking about wanting to meet Paul Stanley to tell him how much I liked his book. He ended up coming by a day or two later to visit Bob and give him a little hell for never having worked with KISS.

Paul was introduced to us and said, "Oh, Black Veil Brides! I didn't recognize you without your makeup!" I laughed and told him how much I liked his book and took a picture with him. He was amiable and seemed very genuine. I'm sure Gene didn't have any problem with us either; it was more my sensitivity and bravado.

As much as KISS and the Misfits were influential to Black Veil Brides overall and with the makeup specifically, we were often compared to Mötley Crüe, as well. Granted, we wouldn't have looked out of place next to them in their *Shout at the Devil* era.

I was intrigued that I'd never gotten any word from Nikki Sixx in the early days of my career, considering how we looked and what people called me. By time we released *We Stitch These Wounds*, I already knew I wasn't interested in being known as "Andy Sixx."

It didn't make sense for me to switch it altogether since I had built this identity, step by painstaking step, on the internet, and the people who *did* know my name before that first album came out knew me only as Andy Sixx. But before our debut album came out, I made a subtle but important change in the liner notes, from "Sixx" to the number "6."

In the summer of 2011, shortly before the release of the second Black Veil Brides album, *Set the World on Fire*, I saw a Tweet where Nikki publicly addressed the existence of "Andy Sixx" for what was, to my knowledge, the first time. Someone asked him how he felt about Andy from Black Veil Brides using his last name or whether or not I was, in fact, his real-life son. He replied with something along the lines of "no, my kids have their own thoughts" or "my kids would be more original than that."

As we were about to release our first big record with a major label, the one that would have the most promotion behind it till that point, I knew this was my chance to make the change altogether. It needed to happen now if it were ever going to happen. It would have been embarrassing to "announce" a name change down the road. (I suppose Sean Combs pulled that when he went from "Puffy" to "Puff Daddy" to "P. Diddy" to "Diddy.")

I saw the Tweet from Nikki and thought, "Okay, he's upset about it. And I'm not thrilled about it either." So why shouldn't I "officially" change it? So, I wrote something up about why it was the right move. I was candid. The name didn't inspire me anymore; it wasn't genuine.

And I'm proud of where I came from and our family name.

Often, I feel like stage names are indicators that someone needs some distance from their parents or even just their upbringing in general. But I *never* felt that way.

I posted this thing on Myspace about how I'd start going by Andy Biersack and why. In the liner notes for *Set the World on Fire*, I was listed as Andy "Six" Biersack, as a way to make the transition with the fans. John Mellencamp, the multiplatinum singer from Ohio's next-door neighbor, Indiana, went by Johnny Cougar from the late seventies till the early eighties. Johnny Cougar was a name sort of forced on him by the music industry. After he'd scored some hits, he had the leverage to start going by his real name. In between, there were a few years where he went by John Cougar Mellencamp,

Our first magazine cover arrived the same year. *Kerrang!* put my face on a 2011 issue with the tag line: *"BLACK VEIL BRIDES. IS ANDY SIXX THE NEW GOD OF ROCK?"*

So, my name was still "Sixx" in the press, regardless of my effort to reframe the narrative. I started hearing that there was tension about it in the Mötley camp. (Our attorney, Dina, represented guitarist Mick Mars around that time.) The unrest was understandable. We were the "hype" band with considerable new momentum behind us. As one might imagine, the *last* thing I wanted was to have any sort of problem with Nikki Sixx.

The Sunset Strip Music Festival was coming up in August 2011, and we were on the Saturday bill headlined by Mötley Crüe. I hoped that Nikki and I could sit down together that day and talk it over. I wanted to explain my position and history with the whole thing and to make it clear that I was never trying to "steal" anything from him or his band.

To my surprise, he wasn't interested in talking about the name Andy Sixx. He did sit down with me. But he offered financial, songwriting, and career advice, instead.

He told me how much I should set aside from every check, that he imagined we were about to become much more prominent, and a few things he wished people had told him early on.

As he recounted himself in an interview with *Sleaze Roxx* conducted a few months later, "I've told them they are missing one thing and need to write [something like Alice Cooper's] 'School's Out' or 'Shout at the Devil.' They've got to write that anthem to unify everyone, as everyone wants to like them, but they just haven't proven themselves yet. BVB have good songs, but they don't have *the* song yet, but that takes time."

Nikki and I never discussed the name "Andy Sixx" ever. We became friendly with each other for a good while after that. I went on his radio show, *Sixx Sense*, a few times. We texted each other. He sent me photos of interesting buildings he saw on tour.

We don't talk so much anymore, but I'm sure if I saw him, there wouldn't be any negative vibes. He's always said very encouraging and positive things about Black Veil Brides. When we recorded with Bob Rock, he made sure to let him know he was excited we were working together. Nikki Sixx came in and out of my life, and he was very kind.

Dee Snider from Twisted Sister is another hard rock icon with whom I had that type of friendship. We'll still talk from time to time. Sebastian Bach became intensely involved in my life for a moment. Beyond the *Golden Gods*, Alice Cooper made very flattering high-profile mentions of Black Veil Brides, from Westwood Radio shows to *Rolling Stone*.

We aren't in touch anymore, but as recently as 2017, a friend told me Alice mentioned us on his radio show. I suppose it's the nature of rock friendships; they burn brightly for a moment, and then eventually, they sort of fizzle. It's challenging to maintain that intensity.

I've been very fortunate not only to meet so many of my heroes but moreover to have such positive experiences with them. Sure, there were a few experiences that were less than excellent, but they could have been much worse, I suppose.

Marilyn Manson and Glenn Danzig were two guys I was never excited to meet because I knew enough about each of them not to expect more than the cold shoulder.

The different times I was put in front of each of them, my instincts proved to be correct. Alice brought me over to Manson at the *Golden Gods* and introduced us. Manson just said something dismissive like, "Okay…" then abruptly turned around and ignored me.

Kevin Chiaramonte did publicity for both Danzig and Black Veil Brides around the same time, so he took me into Glenn's dressing room to say hello to him and Doyle. As I was walking out, I overhead Danzig make some quick dismissive comment about me. It was an indication that he figured me for a creepy fan all up in his personal space.

I can laugh about the Street Dogs story now because I'm not even sure I've gotten it right. I can only remember it from my perspective; I do recall with vivid clarity how it made me *feel*. Granted, I was an awkward kid who was undoubtedly hypersensitive about it.

Surely I've seemed rude or insensitive to a fan at some point without meaning to. The important thing is always to make an effort because those impressions will last.

We've firmly established how much I hate to be dismissed by now, right?

I won't ever purposely dismiss a fan.

22

WHISKEY & WINE

THE TIMES I'VE BEEN less than my best self to a fan, a contemporary, or a stranger have almost always involved alcohol. It's strange that I ever became so carried away with drinking because I never developed a genuine love for it. It never felt like *me*.

Deep down, I always saw myself as the classic teetotaler. Most of my heroes became sober or never took a drink in the first place. Gene Simmons has rather famously never done drugs or gotten drunk. Magician and comedian Penn Jillette doesn't imbibe, either.

I essentially faked my way through drinking and smoking during my teenage years. I "smoked" cigarettes but didn't inhale them. I honestly hated alcohol and tobacco, but I had so little social interaction before meeting these band guys from Southern Ohio and Northern Kentucky, I figured it was a "requirement" to have any credibility with them. (Eventually, I inhaled my cigarettes and became hooked on them.)

In the early days of the Compound, I became pretty good at pretending to drink. I'd put a bottle to my mouth and fake a gulp. Once I felt the buzz from vodka, drinking became more than make-believe. I realized I could self-medicate to ease my obsessive anxiety.

I was in Los Angeles and in a band that was gaining momentum. People who were in bands I knew came over to the Compound to party. It was all part of the ladder to success and recognition with my music, my art. There wasn't any room for my social awkwardness or feelings of isolation to slow me down. Alcohol seemed like a cure.

I appreciated the lowering of my inhibitions in conversation. I enjoyed a certain level of numbness. I wasn't consciously putting it in those terms, but that's what happened.

Around the time we did our first headlining tour in 2009 or thereabouts, I got really into whiskey. There was never a time I worried I couldn't function without it, but I became increasingly married to the idea that "this is part of what we do."

I know that I never had a drinking "problem." People can sit in front of me and have all of the drinks in the world, and it doesn't tempt me to join them. I've personally just never really liked it. I've always found drunkenness obnoxious, even when I was drunk myself. I just figured, "We're this crazy hard-partying type band. Drinking is part of what we do."

When we made *Set the World on Fire,* I was in the throes of trying to be as *rock 'n' roll* as possible. Our producer wasn't always around, but he did turn up from time to time to give us a few tidbits of "wisdom." One such nugget was the idea that my singing sounded much better when I was drunk. I often came to the sessions with a bag from the inside of a box of wine slung over my shoulder like bagpipes.

I went into nearly every song on every record after that with a singer's version of the traditional "hot toddy": whiskey, Throat Coat medicinal tea, and honey. I didn't get falling down drunk in the studio, but I was always drinking.

From there, it was easy to develop the romantic notion that alcohol helped to open up my mind, so I started opening a bottle of red wine when I sat down to write lyrics.

During the making of the self-titled album in Vancouver, I often sat alone in my hotel room, where I would kill an entire bottle while drafting words to the songs. I was convinced I couldn't work, couldn't create, or do anything meaningful otherwise.

Naturally, it took a physical toll. I wasn't eating well. I got sick more often.

The wine, the whiskey, the vodka, it would all serve to silence my deeper concerns, my feelings of isolation, and "otherness" in groups of people, my nagging anxieties.

The drunker I became, the less I would "hear" those things in my head. As is often the case for many people,

I built up a tolerance, which meant it would take more alcohol to get there. By the time we made our fourth record, I would get blackout drunk. Blackout drinking and the exhaustion from the longer and more extended periods of touring gave way to severe depression. I found myself sitting alone in hotel rooms, thinking, "I never used to feel *bad* about my life, the choices I've made, or myself in general. Ever." It was terrible.

Weed made me feel sick. The pharmaceuticals people use recreationally—OxyContin, Diazepam, muscle relaxers, sedatives, and whatnot—those were never my drugs of choice. Even after Hollywood & Highland, I didn't care to take my prescribed medication.

On Warped Tour that summer, people knew I had Vicodin. Band and crew members from other busses would descend upon me at truck stops trying to buy it. They'd knock on the door and be like, "I heard you guys have a stash of Vicodin in here."

I've never, ever tried heroin. I've heard of friends using it. I've known people who have done it. I've never actually seen someone with it. I never witnessed a person smoke crack until 2017, when my security guard and I saw some people freebasing cocaine in an area of Vancouver called "Blood Alley." The number of people I'd ever seen smoking crack went from zero to about twenty-five from the time we left the bus till we returned.

Our security guard, Matt Yanni, started working with the band in the summer of 2011. Over the years, he and I built an unparalleled friendship and brotherhood. Every minute of the band's rise, Yanni was there. He was with me when I fell in love with Juliet.

My grandmother calls Yanni her "guy" in a loving way, a sentiment echoed by my entire family. Yanni is a genuinely kind-hearted person, and I consider myself lucky to have spent so much of my life and career with him by my side. He saw me at my highest and lowest points and protected me not only from potential physical dangers but from the emotional turmoil I've faced on tour, including loneliness.

The most shocking thing I learned about cocaine is that its use is much more casual than I'd have ever guessed as a kid. I always had this trepidation about it. Then I get involved in the entertainment industry, and I see all of these people, including very successful people, sniffing cocaine. I'll never forget the first time someone offered it to me. "Do you want any of this?" I thought, "Wait a second. You're not a 'kingpin.' You're just a guy!"

Unbeknownst to me for a long time, the alcohol was covering more than my anxiety. It masked physical ailments that I would have detected much sooner without the boozy numbness. I suffer from something called Piriformis syndrome, a disorder of this narrow muscle that's part of the lower back, near the butt, which was only aggravated by jumping off guitar cabinets, drum risers, speakers, monitors, and stages for years.

As it began to catch up with me, I could sense some physical changes beneath the thick layer of drunkenness. One indicator was that I had I started putting most of my weight on my right hip, which made me stand a bit strangely.

THEY DON'T NEED TO UNDERSTAND

It became evident in photos. I made excuses. I told people one of my legs was longer than the other, though no doctor had ever said that to me. It was something I invented as an easy way to change the subject.

Eventually, I felt pain all over my body. By late 2013, without knowing, I'd essentially cut off the entire muscle group in the lower right half of my back due to all of the unconscious shifting with my back, hips, and legs. It didn't so much atrophy as it sort of gave up.

The Piriformis muscle group is essential to our posture, our core. Mine was being strangled, which brought on other changes, like my blood cell count.

By spring 2014, it took away much of the feeling in my legs.

It was terrifying. It pushed me to seek out some proper medical attention finally. I couldn't ignore the chronic pain or the injury from Hollywood & Highland if I couldn't walk. I started with a general practitioner, and because it was the lower half of my body, I also went to a urologist.

All of that squeezing of a particular muscle group changed the way my blood cells were able to pass through, so the doctors looked at all of these test results and determined I must have some sort of bloodborne illness. Before long, they had me essentially radiating myself from the inside out with these crazy medicines to eliminate a bloodborne pathogen it turned out I didn't have. I went to see several types of doctors before I ended up with the specialist who misdiagnosed me. They prescribed an incredibly high-strength drug that made me feel as though I'd lost my mind. It turned out that it drove some users to suicide. (The drug is now off the market.)

A sports medicine doctor or physical therapist that works on athletes would have had a better chance of recognizing what was happening, I suppose.

I didn't eat or sleep well, and I drank heavily. I had to cancel some shows in South America. I actually flew to Cincinnati to see a specialist, who prescribed me some medication, and then I went immediately back on the road and resumed the tour.

Juliet was in Nashville, making a record. I hung around with people that enabled my drinking. I got into behaviors that were not representative of me, but I couldn't remember them anyway. Given the alcohol and the medication, I was like a shell of a person.

And remember, by the time we made our fourth album, I had stupidly convinced myself that I had to be drunk to be at my best creatively. I figured drinking an entire bottle of red wine while writing lyrics was part of this essential process required for artistic greatness.

What's funny is that alcohol actually began to dissolve my sense of connection with the creative side of myself. I didn't realize at the time that I was substituting much of the obsessive-compulsive behavior from my childhood— "I need to flush this toilet thirteen times in a row or something bad will happen"—with this rock 'n' roller binge drinking lifestyle. "I need to have a shot before I can sing. I need to have some wine to go onstage."

I was continually drinking when we made *Wretched and Divine*. I was on a steady diet of alcohol and (for some reason) green olives. That lifestyle likely contributed to an inflated feeling of being in a creative flow. But as we began to make a plan to record the follow-up, I was in the throes of numbness from this medication for an illness I didn't have.

When we entered the preproduction stage for album number four, I didn't have many ideas for lyrics or themes. After *Wretched and Divine*, I'd become hung up on the idea that a "story" was essential. Not so much a "concept" but some kind of outline in my mind, which I could dedicate myself to executing, with a beginning, middle, and end.

I wondered during the preproduction process, "When will I come up with something great?" Making *Wretched and Divine* felt so fluid. Every day was a new adventure. Would I be able to make something equally impressive in my current state? Every strong piece of art I've done I've been able to put into the context of the larger story that I'm telling. To answer the question: "What is it that I'm trying to achieve here?"

I'm furious on that fourth record, and not in an artistically beneficial way. I was just miserable to be around. I never finished recording a song with that euphoric feeling from a job well done. I felt "good" about the songs but couldn't achieve that transcendence so essential to turning something good into something great. I've written songs in my life that I recognized as special as soon as I finished them. That was missing for me, and as a result, I've never had a significant emotional attachment to that album.

I just didn't feel like I had a story when we started working on the self-titled record, and even now, I'm not sure that I ever arrived at one. Don't get me wrong. I know that the album is *genuine*. There isn't a moment on the album where I phoned it in. It's earnest. But listening back to it a few years later, I have to confess that it's not my favorite work.

There are some overwhelmingly positive things about *Black Veil Brides*. It was important for the band to make a record together where I wasn't steamrolling over everyone with my grand ambitions and thematic master plan. It was a lesson I needed to learn.

As much as I enjoy *Wretched and Divine,* working on that album was a tumultuous time within our ranks. I was so adamant and driven that I wasn't sensitive to input or opinions from the other members of the band. That's not a healthy way to operate, at least not within the context of a group. It's more appropriate for a solo artist.

One thing I've realized about myself is that if I'm building a house of cards with someone, I'll add my card, the person will add a card, then I'll immediately knock it over and start again because the other person has "ruined" what I was putting together. It's a part of my personality I'm not proud of, and I've worked on improving it.

If I'm going to be in a band, then I need to let it be a *band*. I need to be a member of the group, and we all need to share the space and respect each other completely.

Bob Rock is one of the kindest people I've ever worked with. I mean, he's a Canadian who lives in Hawaii, what more is there to say? He's incredibly sweet. And it was magical to be able to get on the phone with a journalist at *Kerrang!* who'd written *books* about Metallica and hear these amazing stories. We used the same board as the *Black Album*.

In addition to the time in Vancouver, we worked on the album at Henson Recording Studios, in the heart of Hollywood, at the former A&M Studios. Charlie Chaplin was the first occupant of that studio space in 1917. It was the headquarters for A&M Records starting in the late sixties; the company founded by the late Jim Henson, creator of The Muppets, took it over in 2000. Herb Albert and Phil Spector worked there in the sixties. The Doors, John Lennon, and Cheap Trick were among the icons who recorded there in the sixties. The eighties saw Bruce Springsteen, Pink Floyd, the Ramones, KISS, and Bob's friends in the Cult and Bon Jovi. Nineties visitors included Soundgarden, Guns N' Roses, Korn, No Doubt, the Rolling Stones, Dr. Dre, and Stone Temple Pilots.

Not only did we work in the same places with much of the same gear as Metallica had on the *Black Album*, but we also used a lot of the same backup singers that had been on Bob's albums. There was rock 'n' roll magic happening every day during the making of that album. Our more stripped-down songs were written primarily in a rehearsal space. Bob wanted to make sure we'd demoed everything and could play the songs together well. It was a much more traditional way to write and record than we had ever done before.

I recorded my vocals to analog machine into Pro Tools with a handheld microphone, like I would do live, singing each song all the way through every time. I didn't sing a line, take a breath, and sing the next line. Bob and his engineers weren't interested in punching everything in. You can hear some vocal fatigue in certain songs. It's very raw.

As a whole, however, I'm afraid the experience of making the album outweighed the actual finished product. In some cases, we spent more time being excited about how cool it was to make a record that way than on the actual songs themselves. I was also in a very dark place, drinking to excess. I'd plow through a bottle of red wine each day.

While Black Veil Brides is not my favorite of our records, it does have some of my favorite songs. "Faithless," "Goodbye Agony," "World of Sacrifice," "Devil in the Mirror." Those are songs that accomplished what I wanted to say with them. I mean, there are more good songs than bad on that album. But then there's something like "Sons of Night," which became a bonus track. It's a bit nonsensical lyrically. I have no idea what I was trying to say with that one. That was part of the whole "rock 'n' roll" idea, I suppose.

I take full responsibility for those moments. I didn't have the emotional stability to sit down and write something as straightforward and well thought out as "Faithless" every time. I can listen back to "The Shattered God" and feel happy with the story I told in that one.

Overall, working with Bob Rock was terrific, the time in my life was dark, and the tour behind that album was the worst emotional situation I've experienced.

I'm not using alcohol as an excuse. We are all responsible for our own choices, and I chose to drink. That choice led to others. I'm obsessed with things going how I want them to, and it could make it a nightmare to be around me when I added alcohol to the mix. Every angry situation I've had within the band involved alcohol.

Drinking was undoubtedly part of the Golden Gods speech. I had a whole thing planned that I wanted to say about my grandfather. Then the crowd did what they did.

Guns N' Roses challenged many of their media detractors by name in the song "Get in the Ring" from *Use Your Illusion II*. Axl Rose felt slighted, misrepresented, and disrespected. He'd sing that song wearing a catcher's uniform and a kilt onstage. The creativity and artistry involved in fighting back like that were mocked by some but celebrated by many. Sometimes it's something more straightforward, but no less defiant, like Tupac spitting at a photographer's camera or Miley Cyrus sticking out her tongue.

Yet many painted me as awful that time I defended my band against a chorus of boos.

Like most people, I have many sides to my personality. My mom often jokes, "I don't know *that* version of you." When video surfaces with me joking around with an interviewer, there's always someone who'll say, "I know everybody thinks this guy is a jerk, but look how silly and self-deprecating he is here!" It's funny how they'll strongly feel the need to preface it like that. It all comes back to the 2013 Golden Gods Awards.

A few bands decided to use that moment as a launching pad for some free press with a bunch of sanctimonious and opportunistic posturing about how terrible we are.

The worst was when they'd say, "I don't like how Andy disrespected the fans," because those weren't *my* fans. That was a small horde of people gathered in a modest-sized venue to watch a metal award show headlined by Metallica. That crowd hated us.

I did appreciate it when Robb Flynn from Machine Head went out on a limb to sort of champion us. (After the Golden Gods, he even gave our *music* another chance.)

It's a sad testament to the state of the rock scene that something "dangerous" or "edgy" would be so polarizing and controversial. There's a lot of envelope-pushing in pop and hip-hop music these days, yet suddenly we're supposed to be polite in the rock world?

The specific rock scene we exist in comes with a subculture that can be welcoming. But for a kid whose only exposure to the current climate of rock music is commercial radio, I completely understand why that kid would choose another genre of music over that one.

What was the best thing about that Golden Gods situation? The fans. *Our* fans.

There was no electoral college, no select committee. They gave us that award with their enthusiasm and initiative, ensuring we won more votes than the competition.

I do wish I'd chosen my words more carefully. "Fat bearded assholes?" Ugh.

I reacted, in the most basic way, as a child would respond. My body image ideas created this idea in me that being overweight isn't "rock n' roll." It's not the way a rock star is "supposed" to look. These were all things I had constructed within myself.

When I was a kid, I was very insecure about my weight. I used to think that if I wore a T-shirt that was tight around my neck, it would slim my neck because I felt that I had prominent double chins that kept girls away from me. I was very self-conscious about it. One day a teacher stopped me in the middle of the hallway and berated me about all of the safety pins on my shirt. So, in front of everybody, I had to take them out, revealing to everyone that I had pinned my shirts up around my neck like a bib. I walked away with my shirt collar all stretched and huge from being pinned all day.

While I had the bravado of an adult onstage that night, the truth is, I felt embarrassed. It was the same kind of humiliation I'd felt as a kid when people made fun of me. Of course, I had no issues with beards or with someone whose weight was different than mine. We had people on the road with us (including one of my favorite people on the crew at that time, Jeremiah) who more than fit the description of "bigger bearded heavy metal guy."

Every day we were being told the way we looked wasn't okay. When that crowd started booing us because of our makeup or whatever, I felt embarrassed, bullied.

I wanted to say something that would make them feel embarrassed, too.

I was incorrect. I had a lot to learn. And I wasn't talking about anyone in particular. At the NAMM convention the following January, a guy took me aside and said, "Hey, just so you know, I'm that guy you yelled at during Golden

Gods, and I don't appreciate it." I thought, "Boy, I don't know how to explain that I wasn't talking to you." I was lashing out at Cincy Punk dot org, and all of the people like them in my life.

I don't like to watch the videos from that night. It doesn't feel like me. In more recent years, I was in a meeting where someone brought it up. "Oh, that was so great!" I have to smile and go, "Yeah, crazy times!" But the truth is I have no pride in acting like a jackass at a fan-voted metal award show a few years into my career on the heels of what would prove to be our most commercially successful record to date.

It's the antithesis of my public personality nowadays, as anyone who tunes into *The Andy Show* or has seen me hosting similar events can attest.

The day after that Golden Gods, we flew to Arizona to perform at KFMA Day, a radio festival held at Kino Veterans Memorial Stadium, a minor league baseball stadium in Tucson. We were at the fest all day as video of our acceptance speech at the *Golden Gods* started blowing up on the internet. I was still drunk from whatever alcohol was in my system by the time I got back to my hotel room, where I wrote this:

May 5, 2013
1:00 a.m.
Tucson, Arizona

If you'll indulge me, I'd like to start this by posing a hypothetical. Let's say, for the better part of your life, you've been different in some form or fashion. You, as a person, tend to stray from the conventional, and this often causes you to be at odds with most of the society and culture around you.

Throughout your time on this Earth, your general well-being is often predicated on your ability to survive and flourish. The world outside is often so dark and empty, so as you go, you run to build your defenses. The basic idea is in no way uncommon or even reserved for "different people." It's innate in all forms of life. Protect yourself so that you can continue to live, learn, and grow as a being.

With that self-preservation in your arsenal, you go out into the world. You go to school or work or often even home, and you're persecuted. But you've had this eternal dam that you've built to protect your heart from negativity. What happens to dams, when the water rushes too hard and fast?

The dam breaks.

We all have those moments where we had just had it. We've had it with what they say, what they've done, and how they act. They, of course, can be anything from your neighborhood bully to your boss or even sometimes a loved one. We explode, right?

Let's get back to my hypothetical. You were standing with your best friends in the world, and you've just been notified that something that you've all worked so hard on, and had put so much of yourself into, is receiving an award. You feel so proud and elated, particularly when you are "different." It's a hell of a feeling to know that something you've done may have connected so strongly with other "different" people in the world.

But that's after you find out that you're being honored in this way. You were sent into a room. You enter the room, and it's full of people. These are people who don't know you, haven't laughed with you, cried with you. They have shared no pain or joy with you, and though you're eager to share your newfound joy with them, they suddenly begin to show you that they hate you and your friends.

They do not agree with the notion of awarding your hard work, and they are actively openly telling you as much. By cursing, booing, wagging middle fingers, etc. How do you feel? Not necessarily how do you react, but how do you feel? It's easy for me to sit and act poetic about the justification of behavior and how something I, or any of my friends, have done is just right and genuine.

But I want to ask you, my friend, my fellow different people, would your dam come bursting down? Would you feel an overwhelming sense of anger toward those who are aggressively attacking your very existence? Are you doing the thing that you're most passionate about in this world? Do you think you could find yourself defensively yelling back? Maybe even saying things you regret or throwing the attacks that they have back at you? The attacks on your appearance, on your life...

If you think maybe you could, or would, feel that way, I can relate.

I know that sometimes I'm a loudmouth, and, yes, one can accuse me of loving the sound of my own voice. But it's because, when the world outside didn't want me, I built myself into something I could be proud of. Necessity is the mother of invention. A lonely kid who, instead of going out to play with the mean kids, would rather make KISS costumes and sing Misfits songs, has to find ways to forge an identity and create a new environment.

I've always firmly believed that we could be anything we want to be in this life. I'm a kid from Cincinnati who used to get my ass handed to me every day for how I chose to express my creativity. Yet I've been able to find this community of people that allow me to make music for a living and to tour the world. It's pretty damn cool, and I reflect on that fact often.

I've been different all my life. And like so many of you, I continue to pay the price for that. But I refuse to let other people's opinions of me, or my band, change the way that I live. I will continue to make music with my friends. I will continue to sing this way, look this way, and act this way.

Sometimes, when the world outside pushes you too far, I think it's OK to [push back].

In the words of one of my biggest inspirations and heroes, Dee Snider:

We're Not Gonna Take It Anymore.

Andy.

23

JULIET

WAKING UP IN A cold puddle of my urine was a genuine crossroads.

Like that infamous night at the Golden Gods, there were times when I'd find myself on stage, at a festival or tour stop, when someone would flip us off. I should have had no problem getting past it, but the part of me that said "this is not how the show is supposed to go" was only amplified by drunkenness. There's an impulsive, reactionary part of me that is willing to steer the ship onto the rocks just to teach the fish a lesson.

It's not a pleasant way to live because it involves near-constant frustration. It's not fun for the people that I care about to be around, either. (Plus, the time I mooned the audience at Download Festival in the UK revealed that I, in fact, had no butt to show.)

I awoke in my London hotel bed, covered in piss, after the 2015 *Kerrang!* Awards show, where I'd gotten literally "piss drunk." After cleaning up, I went down to the lobby to meet up with Chris Holley, who had become our guitar tech a few months prior.

I'd resolved to quit drinking a couple of times before, but that time I knew it had to stick.

I could have quickly spiraled further into depression and self-doubt, but Chris talked me down. We had a conversation filled with clarity and emotional depth, and it wasn't the first time since he'd come on the road with us. He'd become an advocate of me getting my life back on track, and I was the same for him. We wanted the best for each other.

We'd known each other for less than a year by the time we got to London, but we'd become pretty close. During that hotel lobby conversation, we talked at some length about keeping one another accountable, encouraging each other to be at our best.

We connected and established a plan of sorts to transform our daily lives. That day, we hit the gym together for the first time. As I sweated out a noxious combination of vodka and regret, we resolved to give up alcohol, exercise more, and dedicate ourselves to becoming better people. We flew home to the States the following day.

I was exhausted but optimistic when I got off the plane at LAX, excited to see Juliet and to enjoy the relative comforts of our home. Once in bed, I fell asleep in seconds.

I was awakened the next morning by a phone call. Chris was dead.

Chris passed away in his sleep June 14, 2015, in a Los Angeles hotel room.

As I wrote to our fans: "There's no way I could convey the sadness that it brings to share with you all the passing of our friend and brother, the beautiful and kind Chris Holley. Chris has worked for us as a guitar tech for only a short time but has quickly become one of my best friends in the world. As one of the most sincere and passionate human beings I have ever met, it is not hard to understand why he has touched the hearts and minds of so many…Chris was one of a kind and will forever be missed. We lost a musician, a friend, and a true brother."

I wrote "Beautiful Pain" about him, as that is what I felt around his family. It's what I felt going through my phone and looking at old pictures of him, reading our text thread.

"Beautiful Pain" describes something past the point of the initial shock and the mourning that follows. It's that combination of happiness and sadness we feel in our stomachs when we remember a great experience with someone we loved while simultaneously adjusting to the reality that person is now lost to us.

Losing Chris screwed me up. The conversations we had in England encouraged me to turn away from self-loathing and self-destruction and back toward something positive. I felt in my gut that we would be close friends for a long time. Yet less than forty-eight hours later, he was gone.

There are people in the world who have experienced a loved one dying brutally. The death I've been around has been mundane and, therefore, even more alarming and real to me. Chris died after a long flight I take myself about five times per year. "Beautiful Pain" doesn't deal in sweeping imagery of grand battles, monsters, demons, or religious iconography. It's about the reality of how I feel about mortality.

Chris and I had made a pact, and I had to see it through. I kept my word.

I needed to grow up and deal with the fact that I'm anxious all of the time, accept that things may often upset me, and focus more on what makes me happy and fulfilled.

In life, terrible things happen. We make mistakes. People disappoint us as we disappoint others. Why make those situations worse by adding alcohol, teetering just at the edge of bad decisions and unfortunate circumstances? I wanted clarity and to be a better version of myself. I want to have all of my wits about me to be able to make the best decisions I can. I want to always feel like myself, no matter the circumstances.

I did Warped Tour entirely sober for the first time in 2015 and decided I'd just keep going. I didn't join Alcoholics Anonymous or go to rehab. I just stopped.

The debut Andy Black Album, *The Shadow Side*, was the first album I made sober.

Feldy told me my voice sounded much better without the alcohol. My range was bigger, my delivery stronger. (Plus, I was more enjoyable to be around.)

When I made my first solo song, "They Don't Need to Understand," I was pretty unhappy. There were elements within the band I wanted to distance myself from as much as possible. I needed a lifeline, a way out. I couldn't figure out how to fix the scenario from the inside; I was bound by personal and legal obligations, with no clear solutions.

I refused to give up on music. Feldy and I started messing around with some other styles. The stuff we wrote together at first was maybe too "on the nose" in terms of eighties style pop-rock. But making music like that together was fun. It was during Grammy week, in February 2014, when I sat down with the label and told them I'd like to make a solo album.

I explained that the band was a bit burned out after all of the back-to-back records and tours and that I wanted to experiment with a more synth-based sound. The label suggested I just fire all of the band members and turn Black Veil Brides into a synth-rock solo project instead. I was very offended. They didn't understand Black Veil Brides at all.

It was a ridiculous suggestion and a bit of a cliché record label mistake, the kind of error in judgment that can send a person's life way off course without really affecting the company. It was a stupid idea, and I was never going to allow that to happen. I was bound to them contractually, which meant they had the first right of refusal to anything I wanted to do. They'd said no to Andy Black, which meant I couldn't make money with it elsewhere.

But I realized I could still release solo music, so long as nobody made money from it. I decided to release a single song as more of a "soundtrack" to a YouTube video. We contacted Hot Topic and offered them the video and related merchandise. Pat and I filmed "They Don't Need to Understand" in the parking lot at Richard's gallery and walking around in that neighborhood on Fairfax in Los Angeles. The video did exceptionally well online, so lo and behold, suddenly the label was very interested in Andy Black after all.

The Shadow Side demonstrated my fuller understanding of the positive things I have in my life and my ability to put how I feel about the good stuff into songs. I can find happiness while still accepting that not everything is going to fall together with the way I want it all the time. *The Shadow Side* came together as I settled into this healthier reality.

A certain amount of drama is right for a rock band. It's sort of how we keep each other in check and find the right balance with everything we release. But when I made the solo records, there was no drama. It was a much different process than the band setting.

Artistically there was a real atmosphere of camaraderie and fun. It reignited my passion for making music. Several people came by to work on the album, as cowriters and performers, including Patrick Stump (Fall Out Boy), Gerard and Mikey Way (My Chemical Romance), Ashton Irwin (5 Seconds of Summer), Rian Dawson (All Time Low), Quinn Allman (ex-The Used), Joel and Benji Madden (Good Charlotte), Dean Butterworth (ex-Morrissey), Peter "JR" Wasilewski (Less Than Jake). There were top-tier pop songwriters like Simon Wilcox and Emily Warren, a lot of contributions from Feldy's then engineer and mixer Zakk Cervini and guest vocals from Matt Skiba and Juliet.

Granted, when one has to more or less "trick" a record label into allowing something, that doesn't mean they are behind it full force. Feldy and I decided just to go forward. I remember feeling for maybe a week that perhaps the label would fall in love with it. But ultimately, they didn't seem to understand it. But as dark as the times were before *The Shadow Side*, that was equally as light. It made me love making music all over again.

People like Gerard Way and Patrick Stump coming by to write, sing, and collaborate with us made the experience that much better. My passion for making music renewed.

A few reference points for the record, at first, were The Psychedelic Furs, Sisters of Mercy, Tegan And Sara, and David Bowie, if not so much in sound, in spirit. It was a very personal record. I didn't write so much about leading the charge for the counterculture.

Lyrically, Andy Black is less of a reflection of a position I've taken on something. The lyrics were an insight into my emotional core and demonstrative of my ambition to expand as a storyteller. I love how Bruce Springsteen and Mike Ness paint vivid moving pictures in their music without always offering advice or instruction to the listener. It was just about the feeling. I tried to capture that with songs like "Put the Gun Down."

It's hard to write an ode to your sweetheart over the riffs in "Coffin" or "Faithless." The music on *The Shadow Side* made that easier. "Paint it Black" is about Juliet. We often fight like cats and dogs because we're passionate people. Our friends will laugh at us because we'll have a "heated" argument for like sixty seconds, but then it's over. It seems like we hate every bone in each other's body, but a moment later, it's clear how much we're in love. What can I say? I'm an egomaniac, she's Italian. We're made for each other.

Early into my relationship with Juliet, I watched a documentary about Stan Lee. He was the Marvel Comics legend who cocreated so many iconic superheroes including Spider-Man, Fantastic Four, Hulk, Iron Man, X-Men, and Daredevil, together with fellow giants like Steve Ditko and Jack Kirby. Stan "The Man" Lee was married to his wife Joan for nearly seventy years. They both died at the age of ninety-five—Joan in 2017 and Stan in 2018.

With Great Power: The Stan Lee Story (2010) makes Stan's relationship with Joan a central focus. Sure, there are interviews with Tobey Maguire, Frank Miller, Roger Corman. But the heart of the documentary is this incredible marriage. I came away with the impression that ninety percent of the decisions he made, the things he did, the contributions he made to our culture, were all driven by having his wife and family.

I watched that and thought, "That makes sense to me." I'd never thought of it in those kinds of terms before. In every relationship I'd had prior, we compartmentalized our careers and ambitions. "I do this. You do this." One hand didn't wash the other.

As Juliet and I became more serious about each other, I found myself wanting to achieve more creatively and professionally because I wanted the life we shared to grow larger, more fulfilling, and like most couples, more comfortable and stable.

I had relationships before I met Juliet but never anything that made me want to apply myself so much harder to who I am and want to be as a man, to the art I want to share with the world. In the early days of our relationship, that transformation was transcendent for me. It gave me a newfound sense of purpose, a new reason to persevere.

I never felt like I had anybody that understood me completely as a friend or romantic partner until Juliet and I became a couple. I've had close friends, of course, but never someone who felt like that complimentary puzzle piece where it all matches up.

When I found that person who fits so perfectly, I wanted to spend every day with her. I'm not saying that we are exactly alike. Complimentary differences are crucially important.

Juliet is very driven to improve herself as a musician and songwriter, and she's always been that way. She is determined and focused on getting better at her instrument. She applies herself in terms of practice and technique in ways that I never had.

I would focus on assembling a band, crafting these broader storytelling concepts, building a theatrical presentation, building a platform to make my artistic voice standout. I tried to figure out the finer details of the musicianship side of things along the way. In other words, all of my hard work went toward "getting there." But once

I arrived, it was clear I hadn't done the due diligence to be capable of improving myself once I'd gotten there.

I'd see her warm up for an hour before she sang. She'd challenge herself to hit notes she'd never tried. She would reinvent her lyrical concepts and melodies all of the time.

That was something that I just didn't have. For all of my dedication in so many other areas, I had never adequately applied myself in that regard. I've always obsessed over everything else. But for some reason, singing itself didn't matter as much to me as lyrics, attitude, and presentation. (Of course, my heroes weren't beautiful singers, either.)

I felt limited in my abilities, and it would start to drive me crazy. Time and time again, I'd end up writing things that I simply couldn't sing, and it was endlessly frustrating. (*Wretched and Divine* is made up almost entirely of songs I would struggle with live.)

I'd get piss drunk in the studio and strain like hell to track those songs. I listen now, and I can hear myself battling with notes that are easy for me to hit today. For years we just accepted that the first note of "In the End" was the highest I could ever get. It took an hour for me to get there. But now, through practice and application, I've greatly improved.

I'm sure the fans have noticed that I've become a much better vocalist. Anybody who lives with an exceptional singer, who works hard to sing, is going to have that rub off eventually. A massive amount of credit goes to Juliet for inspiring me to apply myself and work harder at the technique side of what we do.

I credit working with John Feldmann, too. But I can't say enough about living with someone as talented as Juliet and seeing such an exceptional singer work at her craft.

When I met Juliet, I thought, "Wouldn't it be awesome to be with a person like her, a talented artist like her? We could have such incredible conversations." I found her utterly captivating, beautiful, challenging, and thought-provoking.

She was so exciting for me. As I've detailed throughout this book, I often build these scenarios in my head about how I'd like something to go. I knew I wanted to be with Juliet. But the reality of that came with the healthy realization that when it comes to other people, we can't choose how it'll happen with someone else because, ultimately, they are their own person, and they should have the freedom to make their own choices.

In the AFI song "Veronica Sawyer Smokes," from the 2009 album *Crash Love*, Davey Havok sings, "You strayed from my flawless script on which I'd spent a lifetime." Any issues that arose early in our relationship I summoned because of my need to compartmentalize and control circumstances in a way that would fit my narrative.

Like any couple, the problems we had were a result of the scenarios I'd constructed in my mind about how I thought things should go. Once I was able to come to the full realization that life shouldn't operate that way, it was a massive breakthrough for us. She's helped me in significant ways. She's made me more patient. As funny as it sounds, Juliet helped me accept that not everything will happen exactly how I want it to happen.

I'm thrilled to talk about the things I've experienced as a musician, and as a creative person, and to know that's her reality as well. Becoming her husband has made me a better man. It's the best thing that's ever happened to me.

Of course, we are still fiery. We're passionate people. We were both filled with angst. It's tough to be two broke kids in love who are both trying to be rock stars at the same time.

I was on the verge of losing my mind in 2014. Through all of the turmoil and everything we've been through, all of those dark nights of the soul, we stuck it out together. I've reached the point where I simply can't imagine what my life would be like without her.

I'm still on the journey to get to where I'm okay with my anxiety and fear. I have tremendous support from my wife, and she has struggled with some of the same issues. We understand each other in a way that nobody else does in either of our lives.

When it comes to my moral compass and everything else, I'm more like I was as a kid now than at any other point since. I don't have "regrets" so much as I just can't believe some of the behavior I let myself fall into, chasing an idea that I thought would help make me feel more comfortable. I've always had this modicum of discomfort in my social graces, and my obsessive tendencies continue to push me as a creative person.

I wrote about it a lot on *Vale*—my histrionics, my obsessions. "When They Call My Name" is about all of these conversations I've had with Juliet, where I just need her to talk to me and give me peace about the things that make me anxious. (Yes, the fifth album from Black Veil Brides provided a canvas just as broad as *The Shadow Side*, in some ways.)

The obsessions linger, the fear lives on, but at long last, I have started to feel in control.

And I have my best friend, my wife, by my side.

24

THE ANDY SHOW

IT WASN'T JUST VANITY. There was a deeper reason I named my podcast *The Andy Show*.

At least one or two days per week, I become overcome by the fear that I am the central character in either something awful or in something great. I've regularly dreamt up scenarios wherein everything wonderful is happening to me, that all of my dreams are coming true. Ten minutes later, I get hit with the crushing defeat of everything wrong that could ever possibly occur. *People will attack me. Someone is inside my house.*

In these moments, in my mind, I could just as easily win the lottery as I could be run over by a car at any second. I'm not actively thinking about this stuff, but once the thought occurs to me, I'll get wrapped up in breaking it down. I obsess over every element of how it could happen. I overanalyze the scenario until I'm drowning in anxiety.

As the title character in 1998's *The Truman Show*, Jim Carrey's "life" was an elaborate television production watched by millions across the world, known to everyone but him. His friends, family, and coworkers were all actors. Everything in his small town was engineered around him.

As much as it's a fun narrative to write myself into my own *Truman Show*, as I've gotten older, I've found the easiest way to alleviate my anxiety is to remember I am just a regular person. I am trying my best to do good things, help people, and make my loved ones happy.

When I make mistakes, it's not the end of the world. I will not get struck by lightning. When I watch the news and see all of the tumultuous confusion out there or the occasional feel-good report, it helps contextualize my role in everything. I realize how small of a part I play, and frankly, it's liberating.

One of the most immediately comforting things, when I shed the idea of theistic faith, was the realization that it was no longer a necessity to see myself as part of some "bigger plan." Once I was no longer cast as the central character in some narrative, where every decision counts toward whether I'll get into heaven or not, I felt unchained.

I found the idea of the "chaos" more comforting than the idea of a "divine plan." I've struggled with fear, anxiety, obsession, and compulsive tendencies my entire life. I'll think, "I can't throw away these broken mirrors I've had in my house for six months, because when the guy takes it out of the dumpster, he may cut his hand and break the mirror again, which will cause bad luck for both him and me for the injury I've caused."

So I'll put the broken mirrors or whatever in my trunk and fight with myself whenever I'm driving somewhere. "I need just to throw it away. It doesn't make sense to have it."

Robert DeNiro's character in *Silver Linings Playbook* may feel like an exaggerated cartoon to some people. Still, that character was all too familiar to those of us who suffer those types of feelings. For him, it was about doing this or that "correctly" to ensure his favorite team wins. For someone else, it's something different.

Of course, the challenge is that now there are, in fact, people in the world who are very focused on everything I do, thanks to my marginal amount of fame. Some of them obsess day and night about my flaws and mistakes, both real and simply perceived.

In recent years, there have been those who've tracked down where we live, even someone who broke in and rummaged through some Black Veil Brides memorabilia. We've had to pick up and move more than once as a result, which is far from fun.

So that mantra of affirmation that "I'm just one of many ordinary people" gets a little bit tougher when there are people who spend their waking hours attacking me and my wife online. Or they post things on social media attacking my parents or the guys in my band. It's usually over a salacious event that never actually happened or something I said in an interview half a decade ago or whatever. So that anxiety does often return.

But I'm not *the* main character in the world. The world is not, in fact, *The Truman (Andy) Show*. The more I invest myself in what's going on in the socio-political sphere, or the more I quietly contribute to a cause or charity that I know has an unassailable positive impact on the world, the better I feel.

My mom participated in the Women's March on Washington, which filled me with immense pride. Juliet has become more of an activist. It all helped me to contextualize my life in a more realistic and manageable way. I'm a main character for my wife, my family, the fans, and myself. And there are very sinister things going on I can help to fight.

I've built a career centered on singing with the downtrodden. As I entered my late twenties, and it became harder to connect with that angst I felt as a teenager, I broadened my perspective to encompass even bigger battles to fight. I have that "rebel" spirit within me. I'm applying it to much more than the (always necessary, of course) battle against bullies and people that don't understand who we are. It's grown so much more substantial.

At the same time, I have been and remain careful not to get into specific, nuanced detail about my viewpoints concerning politics or religion. I've spoken about blind faith or a lack of any faith, but my number one message has been to question everything and to find your way. That examination could lead someone to Buddhism, Christianity, LaVeyan Satanism, agnosticism, atheism, or elsewhere.

It was a conscious decision early in my career to take a mostly secularist and apolitical stance as an artist. The job for me has always been about exorcising my demons with the things I say and do in a way that could help someone else to do the same thing. I've found that when I listen to music pointed in one direction or the other, it becomes harder to apply the message in the music to my own life.

As much as I respect a strong point of view, I must admit that sometimes I get sick of how much someone "believes" in what they are saying. Having a conviction about something is great. But I tend to tune out someone "preaching" at me.

After the alcohol was gone, some of the compulsive behaviors I'd suppressed returned. The difference is I'm conscious of what's happening and why and I'll make the decision to follow through with some irrational "ritual" type behavior or not. Intellectually I understand the feeling that something terrible will happen if I don't make myself do this or that mundane little thing is silly. But that doesn't mean I won't indulge my OCD a bit.

Some of the compulsive behavior makes me feel comfortable. It's no longer debilitating. As I've gotten older, I've learned to accept that it isn't everything; it's just one component of my personality. I mean to say, when I was in the throes of experiencing something hugely upsetting to me, as I often did when I was a kid, it was more difficult to remind myself that it was merely one element of who I am. I can utilize it, or I can ignore it.

As an adult, now, I'm able to break it down a little bit more and consider, "Well, I know I don't need to do these weird things." I recognize that I don't need to count things in front of me or switch a light on and off a certain number of times or whatever. *If* I do so, it's because I've made a choice to do so and not because it's a "necessity." I realize this isn't ideal, and I am often able to dismiss these sorts of intrusive thoughts and see them for how dumb and inconsequential they are. But other times I'll go ahead with whatever my brain is telling me to do because, well, I just want to be "certain."

We all have our ways of surviving and of getting ourselves through each day. But generally speaking, it's all just life. It's the most mundane situations where the intrusive thoughts of obsessive compulsions confront me. It's not an issue when I'm going onstage; it's an issue when I'm merely lying in bed or taking out the trash.

In other words, it's in the smaller moments. I'll often listen to podcasts to quiet my mind. If I have headphones on and there's music playing, I'll find myself analyzing the lyrics, the song structure, the melodies. It isn't the escapism that I need in those moments. I can listen to a conversation where two people are talking about a football team and escape myself that way; I focus on their conversation rather than having my own.

Very often, I'll listen to something that I completely disagree with and it won't bother me at all because I know it's just a podcast. I don't need to obsess over what is said or how the host's voice sounds. It's just a way of taking my mind off of my mind.

Of course, I do listen to my music when I'm making it because that's an essential part of the process. I want to analyze and reassess what I'm doing before the world hears it. Generally speaking, once something has been released, I won't listen to it again unless I'm relearning something for an upcoming performance. Before the street date, however, I'll listen to something constantly because I'm mindfully analyzing it.

"Oh, that's cool" or "I like that" or "perhaps I should have changed this part." It's a fascinating internal conversation to have. Because once it's out there, it's truly finished.

When is a piece of art ever really done? Once you've given it to the public to consume. At least that's how I look at it. I don't know that I thought *Vale* was "completed," I just figured fifteen months was probably more than enough time. I wasn't trying to turn it into Black Veil Brides' version of *Chinese Democracy* with endless sessions and delays. I could have easily driven myself crazy with continuous writing and editing and rewriting.

One thing I learned making *Vale* is that to move forward, often we must look back.

25

PROMISES & VOWS

As I listened back to the mixes for our band's fifth album, *Vale*, I found myself increasingly reflective about the records that came before it. In so many important ways, my life was completely different than it was when we recorded *We Stitch These Wounds*.

It's even more profound than the changes in my everyday lifestyle. It's down to the things I think about and the way I feel about certain things in the world. Piss and vinegar drenched so much of the first Black Veil Brides album. There's that thirst for revenge and confrontation evident throughout the lyrics, the music videos, and the costumes.

Set the World On Fire carried that spirit forward and refined it. It was our first major-label album, our potential commercial breakthrough. I had more to prove than ever. If there's one sentence that sums it up thematically, it would be, "I'm going to show everybody."

Wretched and Divine was not only a conceptually driven album with grandiose ambition, spinning a fantastical tale incorporating elements of so many subjects that have long fascinated me. *The Story of the Wild Ones* was more importantly, at its heart, about aspiration. And it was about what we pursue and what ultimately pursues us.

The self-titled fourth album was the sound of a lead singer clinging to whatever semblance of sanity he had left. It's the total of my anger and confusion, of my resentments and hostility. In that sense, it's a natural combination and distillation of what had come before. But I wasn't reaching higher. I didn't challenge myself to become *better*.

Going into *Vale*, I was determined to truly encapsulate and magnify the greatest strengths of the Black Veil Brides catalog and reinvigorate the broader themes of what this band represented while at the same time wrapping up a significant chapter.

I certainly wasn't short on inspiration in the years since *Black Veil Brides*. Between my revelations and transformation and the state of the world at large, there was no shortage of things to write about, which inspired me to challenge myself.

Things that happened to me and things I saw around me felt simultaneously like the end of something and the beginning of something else. I realize it's a cliché to say that when one door closes, another one opens, but it's true.

Vale was an endpoint. Conclusions by nature are dramatic. In even the most objective of senses, it was clear to me that we'd arrived at the perfect moment to draw the story arc we'd written across four albums to a dramatic conclusion on the fifth. The future was unwritten. Whatever followed in the wake of *Vale* would be a brand-new chapter.

Less than a week after we completed *The Shadow Side*, Jake and Jinxx said they were ready to get started on the next Black Veil Brides record. We began work on what would become *Vale* before I'd even started to tour behind *The Shadow Side*.

At the time, I felt like *Vale* would be the final Black Veil Brides album. I never said that publicly, but it certainly could have ended up that way. It's like a TV show that may or may not get renewed; I didn't want to leave things with a cliffhanger. If the band could continue past album five, great, but if not, I tried to wrap it up with a strong sendoff.

The last song on the record, "Vale (This Is Where It Ends)," was my goodbye to this thing that I poured my heart and soul into since before I learned to drive a car. It will always be challenging to listen to for me. The first time I played it for my parents, I cried. I had written it, performed it, and recorded it, yet hearing it back with my parents in the car, I wept.

The whole idea that Black Veil Brides might end broke my heart. Some elements felt like immovable objects that we couldn't get past. So, it had to stop. It was heartbreaking, it was terrible, but I didn't see any other way around it at the time.

The songs are very personal to me. I was fully committed to sobriety. I struggled to remember the mistakes I may have made when I was drinking myself into oblivion. I felt delicate, fragile. Overall, *Vale* was really about saying goodbye.

It was also a way to end the storyline I'd begun on *Wretched and Divine*. We made the album separate from one another, for the most part. Jake and Jinxx each recorded in their respective studios. CC recorded his drums with Feldy. Then I recorded my vocals there.

We hardly ever saw each other during that process. It wasn't because we hated each other. The band had just become disjointed. There wasn't a vibrant connection between us creatively so much as there was simply a task to complete. It was so far apart from the way we made *Wretched and Divine*. But it was a crucial album for me.

If *The Shadow Side* was my sobering up and finding happiness, *Vale* was the second wave of emotion that followed. "Well, now that I'm out from all of that, what's next?" If I were to lose what had been the most critical thing in my professional and personal life since I was a teenage boy, what would I do with myself next?

Some fans felt *Vale* was too commercial sounding, which took me by surprise. But in retrospect, I can see that it was a bit more of an "Andy Black Veil Brides" album simply because that was where I was at emotionally and as a songwriter. But I was very proud of that record, and I continue to be very proud of it. It's full of really great songs.

I have a vivid memory of the Warped Tour stop in Atlantic City in 2019. As much as I loved playing in front of all of those people as Andy Black, I found myself wishing it were with my *band*. I didn't want only my initials on the backdrop. I wanted my band back.

The tour cycle for *Vale* included only a handful of shows over about six months. I had a tour bus of my own, away from the rest of the band. I only saw them on stage.

It felt like everything I dreamt about for the band from day one was distorted. It wasn't fun anymore. I know that jobs aren't always "fun," but I refused to live that way. We played some shows at the Roxy in Hollywood, where we were awarded our gold plaques for half a million sales of "In the End," and elements there almost ruined it for me.

I figured I'd make another Andy Black album and simply move on. Sadly, the initial inspiration behind the second Andy Black album was a pragmatic one; I needed to eat. I had to make a living. The band was no longer tenable, and this was my other vehicle. I had very little creative motivation at first. Feldy and I would write things I didn't love.

But then during one of those writing sessions, the phrase "The Ghost of Ohio" came to me. I've long been fascinated by the types of people who are obsessed with nostalgia, who romanticize the past. I know I have personally made revisionist history mentally at times, willfully recalling people and things as better or worse than they were. I started to come up with a story about a character who merely haunts all of the old spots, making up new versions of events to convince himself that everything is just fine.

"The Ghost of Ohio" began as a sparse ballad with just a piano and vocal. I played it for Juliet and some friends and felt like, while the lyrics were great, the song wasn't enough yet. But the ideas were there. The muse had returned. I had something tangible to chase.

Downey and I had begun the process of writing this book, which had me thinking a lot about Ohio and all of the spooky and haunted places I'd spent so much of my time in growing up in Cincinnati. It all coalesced into this concept about *The Ghost of Ohio*.

I pulled a wooden shelf out of my closet and painted this green-faced monster character with an eyepatch. I took a photo of it and sent it to Feldy and Blasko, and everybody agreed: this is the record, this is what we're doing. Let's start over with this new concept.

A friend of ours, Josh Bernstein, contacted me about doing a collaborative graphic novel with the comic book company Z2, who had ventured into similar projects with rock bands. I said, "I wrote a treatment for a comic book just yesterday. So yes, let's do this."

It went from this semi-apathetic march into a second solo album merely to pay the bills into full-blown excitement about new music, a new concept, and a companion comic book.

I love *The Ghost of Ohio*. I got to explore some Bruce Springsteen–style songwriting and other influences that I have. It was my final record in my contract with Universal. I was able to end that relationship on good terms without any anger or resentment. I got to attend San Diego and New York Comic-Con for the first time, promoting my own comic!

I was happy that many of the crew members from BVB's touring crew came with me for Andy Black. I'm so thankful to have met a handful of people through touring with whom I've maintained close relationships. Jesse Lee Butts is undoubtedly among those that I consider family. He's a childhood friend of Robert Murphy, from Illinois. Jesse began as a "do anything" tech for us and worked his way up. First he sat behind the drums, flipping the floodlights on and off. Next he was our drum tech, then production assistant, and eventually merchandise seller. Jesse remains one of my most trusted friends.

In expanding the stage show formalizing the live lineup for the touring behind *The Ghost of Ohio*, I became completely enamored of Lonny Eagleton, an accomplished session musician from Canada who is sweet, humble, and extremely talented. As fate would have it, he was also a massive fan of Black Veil Brides, which he didn't mention for months!

By the end of the touring cycle, as much as I enjoyed it, the itch to play heavier music again grew. I found myself getting angry that I surrendered my band, my passion, because of supposedly immutable circumstances. While I knew the road ahead would be very difficult in terms of repositioning Black Veil Brides to be what we'd intended it to be, I dedicated myself to the idea that we would find a solution. I called up the other guys.

They shared my feelings. We began to talk every day, excitedly texting ideas back and forth while I was still on tour as Andy Black. We'd talked about rerecording *We Stitch*

These Wounds to coincide with the album's tenth anniversary for a long time. By that point, Jake had come into his own as a producer and mixer. I had gotten to know Lonny well through having him in Andy Black. I knew he'd be a perfect addition to BVB.

It was the best time to remake *We Stitch These Wounds* and to create new music to reintroduce the world to this latest iteration of Black Veil Brides, a brand-new chapter.

We conceived *The Night* as a two-song time capsule of sorts. Like, what if we wrote songs that sounded like Black Veil Brides in 2010, with no outside songwriters or producers? We were in between record labels. We didn't need to answer to anyone. The energy Lonny brought to the fold inspired us to bring things back to the band's purest form, too.

One of the riffs came from the period when we made *Wretched and Divine*. It was so intense that I hadn't been able to figure out how to put a melody over it before. The ideas came together quickly for "Saints of the Blood" and "The Vengeance," and the momentum just continued, with several more songs swiftly written to carry Black Veil Brides forward.

Ash Avildsen signed us to his label, Sumerian Records. His belief in me began all of those years ago as the booking agent for Black Veil Brides, the person who introduced us to Blasko, the writer/director who cast me as the lead in his movie and TV show. He supported our idea to accomplish what we wanted to do with *Re-Stitch These Wounds*

We'd always known we could improve on that album. Hardcore Black Veil fans may recall that after *Wretched and*

Divine came out, we tried to launch an online campaign to gather support for us to remake *We Stich These Wounds.* The idea originated from my work with Feldy because he taught me how to access new parts of my voice. We hoped that perhaps the fans would help us put pressure on our previous label to allow us to do it. Ultimately, Standby wasn't interested in having something out there that would compete with their existing release, which is understandable. Most record contracts forbid artists from rerecording anything for that very reason. However, that prohibition tends to expire eventually, as ours did.

CC, in particular, was excited, since he wasn't on that album. We'd also made some tweaks and changes to the songs in the live setting over the years. There are slight alterations to almost all of them. "Never Give In" makes a lot more sense melodically now. Even the songs we didn't change much are bigger and better sonically.

Undoubtedly some fans were disappointed that we took the witch laugh out of the bridge in "Perfect Weapon." Sure, it's not the "Knives and Pens" fans spent a decade listening to, but in our opinion, it's a much better version, and much closer to what we'd always envisioned for it. "Carolyn" was always supposed to be a massive, monstrous rock ballad. It sounded way too small on the first album, so it was a thrill to take another stab at it. From a vocal standpoint, I was a much better singer at twenty-nine than nineteen.

All of those original versions still exist and can continue to be enjoyed. We never told our fans to stop listening to the first album. It was not a replacement for *We Stitch These*

Wounds. It's a companion piece, or a "director's cut," if you will. It's for anyone interested in hearing how we would have intended for that album to sound.

It's our musical version of a #ReleaseTheBlackVeilBridesCut. It was another watershed moment, a dual celebration of an important time for us in 2010 and again in 2020.

26

IN THE END

WATERSHED MOMENTS ARE COMMONPLACE in our society and my daily life. It can be overwhelming. In terms of politics, pop culture, and the like, there's a part of me that misses having the ability to be completely unaware. I miss the freedom to be ignorant. Not because I *am* ignorant but only because with the breadth and availability of information right now, I can't avoid knowing about so many things.

As much as I love having everything at my fingertips because I love facts, there's something to be said for genuinely learning about a given topic versus merely absorbing it. We all seem to know the same things these days, or at the very least, we can.

When I was a kid, I was a big fan of "Weird" Al Yankovic's "All About the Pentiums," his song parody of the Puff Daddy hit "All About the Benjamins." The "Weird" Al version is mostly about computers. It's super fun and silly. At one point, he references the actress Sarah Michelle Gellar. I was eight years old when the song was released. I didn't watch the TV show *Buffy the Vampire Slayer,* so I had never heard of Sarah Michelle Gellar.

Now if there's a "Weird" Al song and he references a celebrity—any celebrity—almost all of us know which famous person he's talking about (regardless of our age) because everyone seems to know everything all of the time about this stuff. It's funny to think there used to be this colossal television show, which my wife grew up loving, that I didn't know anything about whatsoever. I heard "All About the Pentiums" as a kid and thought, "Who the hell is Sarah Michelle Gellar?" I didn't have an iPhone I could use to Google her.

I was able to unplug quite a bit during the Andy Black run on the 2017 Warped Tour. There's something to be said for that, but at the same time, I do want to know things. I like to know everything I can even though so much of the news is so upsetting.

No more drinking, of course, correlated with going out less often. I'll watch a movie and see people drinking, and it just doesn't appeal to me personally anymore. At one point, when I'd first given up alcohol, I'd think, "Man, maybe it would be fun to have a margarita at lunch or whatever," but eventually, I honestly stopped caring about it. I'm not concerned.

249

I mean, I get it. I understand that it's much easier to have a good time around people—especially for someone like me—when there's alcohol flowing through my system. I've always struggled to fit in when it comes to blindly socializing. I love hanging out with people I'm close with or who have interests that intersect with my own. As far as interacting with groups of strangers without the assistance of alcohol, I'm not sure how that would be because I have yet to test myself in that environment.

When I stopped drinking, I purposefully distanced myself from people in my life that weren't healthy to be around. It included those who were enablers, some of whom I realized were sycophants, and others that simply annoyed me on some deeper level.

To each their own, I'm not judging anyone else for how they choose to have a good time so long as it isn't harming anyone else. I just can't fake it without alcohol, and frankly, I don't want to. I don't want to be "seen." I don't need to immerse myself in places like clubs where everyone is yelling in each other's ear and "posed and exposed" in a corner booth hoping to be recognized or in some more fabulous way to be understood.

I'm glad that I experienced many of the things that I did. Even in the heights of the craziest debauchery, I forged positive and meaningful relationships. Perhaps some of them are people I don't talk to often anymore, but I enjoyed their company, and the impact we had on one another as we came in and out of each other's lives was crucial. I made plenty of friends from social circles

I wouldn't have encountered otherwise without the shared "social lubricant" of liquor and, of course, the passion for rock 'n' roll.

I packed in quite a lot in my teens and early twenties—a lot more than I would have without traveling the world playing music. I don't look back on it as some totally harrowing chapter.

But these days I'm remarkably more similar to the kid I was growing up in Cincinnati than the person I became during the relentless ascent of Black Veil Brides I embarked upon with my bandmates after I arrived in Southern California as a young adult.

Considering I am an obsessive person and a bit of a neat freak who thrives on consistency, it's almost unbelievable when I think back to the situations I was in, let alone some of the things I said and did. I mean, was there really a time in my life when I didn't care about doing laundry? I didn't care about things being clean or if I smelled good?

Once upon a time, I wouldn't even plug in a vacuum cleaner. Even in some of the places where Juliet and I lived together early on, I'd smoke cigarettes inside. Irresponsible and thoughtless sort of stuff I couldn't fathom letting myself do now. It's a bit hilarious.

While I made some decisions that weren't good for me, I can confidently say that I always maintained, at least to some degree, what I am in the larger scheme of things.

Amazingly, I was able to hang onto the core of what makes me who I am throughout it all while forging ahead on my career path and ultimately coming back full circle.

I never lost the determination to persevere. I possessed the proper amount of passion for seeing all of it through every step of the way. I wanted to get a message across, to stand for something, to be onstage. I wanted to be a rock 'n' roll star. My dream, so to speak, never changed. Sure, it became clouded from time to time, but it was still there. I made records, and I went on tour. I went out on stage and gave my all.

I just lacked the discipline to be *better*. That's the biggest issue that took over in that period. I grew complacent with my artistry, relationships, family, health, and appearance. I was comfortable to maintain the status quo and do what I'd always done, the same way I'd done it, for at least a year and a half. For someone like me, that can be a type of death. I have always felt driven, and when that started to slip away, I became lost.

I will never go back to being nineteen years old. I'll never be that guy again. As things changed for me and as I crossed over my mid-twenties and closer to my thirties, the renewed elevation of the stuff in my life that is truly most important to me allowed for a new creative space.

The Shadow Side and *Vale* were direct results of that new freedom. Both of them were cathartic in terms of a farewell as certain things drew to a close.

It's not as if I were a wholly different person for half a decade. There were just pieces that were out of place or inconsistent with my priorities and values. I've shed those things, and I've worked harder each day to destroy complacency. Complacency is the enemy of greatness. I've always believed that. I'm still able to dream big and strive for new things.

Recent years have seen significant new "firsts" for me.

The Shadow Side, my first solo album. *American Satan*, my first movie. *The Ghost of Ohio*, my first graphic novel. *Paradise City*, my first TV series. Hosting an award show.

This book.

I'm not ready to call it a day on my grand ambitions. Eventually there's a finite number of things that one can do, but I'm excited to try to get to that "last" first thing. If it makes me happy and if people want me to do something and will allow me to do it by showing up to listen, watch, or whatever the case may be, I have an individual responsibility to deliver.

I'm an entertainer. That is what was given to me. I'm here to uplift people, to make them laugh, to make them upset, to make them hate me. Whatever the situation, I will entertain you. I enjoy helping people escape their problems, even if just for a little while.

I have this vivid memory from my very first day of preschool. It's stuck with me. It takes me back to a central theme of this book and my life. The idea that "I'll show you!"

It was first thing in the morning, and all of the kids were sort of wandering around the room and mingling until the teacher was ready to do whatever she needed to get started. I walked up to the chalkboard and picked up a piece of chalk. I wanted to draw something. I wanted to show everyone my skills. I wanted to show off.

What could I draw that would please everyone in the room? I knew I could draw Bugs Bunny. Everybody loves Bugs Bunny. So I drew this huge Bugs Bunny on the chalkboard. As I proudly scanned the room to see how impressed my new classmates must have been, they met me with an unfamiliar attitude of indifference.

It made me so angry. No reaction? *Tell me you love this Bugs Bunny. Or tell me you hate it and it's the stupidest thing you've ever seen.* Give me something here! I mean, I'd spent minutes drawing it. That's a large portion of someone's life at five years old.

It did not seem fair. Eliciting a response with my art has always been important to me. Even at times when I haven't wanted to admit it, that's still a huge motivator. I crave that reaction. When those kids failed to give me that feedback, I was enraged.

To command any kind of response in any medium I choose will always be a goal for me. In recent years I feed less on the adverse reactions and focus more on positive feedback. The aggressive ones don't get to me. I understand that they are there, but the joy I derive from a positive response means so much more to me than it used to.

I will always aspire to inspire, entertain, and share my art with the world.

I love to sit and contemplate the proverbial "blank canvas." I love the process of making records, starting with nothing, and building something tangible. I love making rock 'n' roll records. I love guitar solos. I love what we do in Black Veil Brides, and I love what I get to do as Andy Black. It's all about the songs.

People act like there's some boogeyman stopping us from achieving more significant commercial success. Yes, the "climate" has changed. But the hunger for music made with authenticity and commitment has never truly waned.

One of the most troubling things about the rock community right now is the general lack, with a few exceptions, of self-reflection and innovation. It's tiresome when I hear bands proclaiming that they're going to "bring back rock music." We should look closer at what was successful in the past and challenge ourselves to improve upon it in some way rather than simply copy from it.

As a kid in Ohio, I'd tell someone I wanted to be in a successful rock band when I grew up, and the response I'd get was usually, "Well, it doesn't work like that."

Well, why not? It worked for somebody. Why can't it work for me, too?

I had to succeed, even though almost no one thought I was going to do well. I don't know that I would've become as successful as I have, or hopefully continue to be, if everybody had said from the beginning, "Oh, this is going to be great!" Because I've always done better in everything I've ever tried as the underdog who overachieved.

There has to be a certain level of self-confidence to believe in something this crazy. Give up on everything else in life to follow a dream like this one against almost insurmountable odds? It takes balls. I give my full salute to any artist, in any medium, who commits to a career in the arts fulltime, let alone for the rest of their lives.

I remain someone who is enamored by the things that I love and enjoy. I have little patience for things that don't interest me. Somewhere along the line, in the middle of my path, the negative influence of alcohol and anger made it so my connection to the things I love dampened. At the same time, my ability to accept unsavory situations dialed up.

I love movies, music, sports, my family. I love working to be a great husband. All of these things were always there, but they were temporarily clouded. I started to prioritize being the drunken guy, the rock star, and the lead singer brooding in a corner somewhere because I felt misunderstood. I allowed those things to become nearly as important as the things I truly loved that initially inspired me.

My resolve has never been stronger. I don't care whether or not the world understands why I love the things that I do. I will continue to embrace them, to fight for them, to hold them close, and to make them my priority. I will throw my entire self behind them.

It could all crash and burn tomorrow. The lucky among us will collect amazing experiences to reminisce about and ponder for the rest of our lives. The most fortunate will even have the chance to continue to create those experiences until the day we die.

I've made grand sweeping statements about how I believe Black Veil Brides can be the biggest band in the world, that we could change things. I think that to do something in this world of music, entertainment, and the arts in general, one has to believe what they're doing is something of substantial significance. Otherwise, what's the point?

Will we see a massive paradigm shift? Will rock 'n' roll bands suddenly become the most popular thing in the world?

I don't know. I don't believe black-and-white televisions or rotary telephones are coming back. Sometimes culture has just moved on.

I do believe that when a band like Avenged Sevenfold has the number one album in the country, the entire rock community should celebrate. So many people will look at a band's latest release and complain that it's not as good as the album that came before, or worse, that the group itself isn't as good as the older bands.

Appetite for Destruction and *The Black Album* are phenomenal masterpieces. Those albums are legendary, undeniable landmarks. But we can't forget that every classic album was once brand new. We can't just *stop*. We have to push forward. What if Guns N' Roses and Metallica had never tried to top the records they had loved themselves growing up?

Why shouldn't young bands have a chance to break through in the same way?

I make enough to live comfortably, but rock music hasn't made me wealthy. There are no delusions of grandeur with me. A lot of people want to feed that myth, to build them up, but I'm not worried about fooling anybody. There are always new horizons to conquer.

People are entitled to their opinions about Black Veil Brides, but when kids come to our shows, they are a part of something. Younger kids dress up in the makeup, the older audience feels a sense of nostalgia about being at a rock show, and they all enjoy the songs. There is something real happening with a lot of other young bands and with us.

In the thick of it, it's hard to see the forest for the trees. Putting this book together, with one of my best friends, allowed me to reflect more objectively on the journey. It's been a wild ride, one equal part joyful and turbulent, to get to where I am now. The majority of the lessons I learned about how to be a moral person despite achieving success at a young age were lessons I learned as a member of Black Veil Brides.

I'm very proud of what we have achieved.

One constant with my public persona, when we started, were those ambitious declarations I'd make to the press about how massive, earthmoving, and gigantic Black Veil Brides would become. "We're going to do *this*! And then *that!*"

There are only a few souvenirs in my home that are representative of my career in music. There's a large frame with four pictures inside of it. One of them contains the first magazine cover my wife was ever on and some clips from the time she appeared in *Vogue*. There's a photo of Twisted Sister front man Dee Snider and myself taken at the Revolver Golden Gods Awards and a headline from a 2011 *Rock Sound* cover story when we were voted "Band of the Year." The quote was, "I believe that we will change music."

I've often found myself looking at that quote hanging there on the wall. Part of me wants to think, "Well, this is disappointing. I certainly haven't changed the music industry since then." But the other part of me knows that in the context of our scene, in our corner of the music world and pop culture, we were instrumental in reintroducing an element of theatricality, showmanship, revelry, opposition, and a type of dangerous excitement.

There were undoubtedly other groups involved in championing those ideas within a genre that had otherwise turned its back on them. I don't believe Black Veil Brides was the "be all end all" with it. But we were indeed part of the vanguard of bands pushing that idea.

We can choose to be disappointed by things if we want to. It's easy to look at something that didn't happen precisely the way that we wanted it to happen and resign ourselves to the idea that we are disappointed. But truthfully, I don't know that I ever had any definitive idea about what specifically was "supposed" to happen for us. I just wanted to *do it*.

I realize the conventional wisdom contends that every twenty-year-old signed to a major label is sold a bill of goods about all of the fantastic things that are in store for them and ultimately will end up bitter and broken because they feel lied to or cheated out of their destiny. I will never be disappointed by the fact that in every year of my life as an entertainer, I've always gotten to do something cooler than I got to do the year before.

I never believed the more fantastical things told to me anyway. I know this will sound hilarious coming from a front man who is known for cocksure and crazy statements like, "*Set the World on Fire* is better than anything Led Zeppelin ever made," or whatever.

But in all reality, that was just my truth relative to my own experience. What I was trying to communicate (and perhaps couldn't articulate precisely the right way) was that Black Veil Brides meant more to *me* than any other band ever had. Making these albums, hearing my own recorded voice, working with A-list rock 'n' roll producers? Knowing how many people are going to listen to this music? Black Veil Brides means more to me than KISS, and it means more to me than Alkaline Trio. It means more to *me*, period.

It's not like Black Veil Brides matters to Led Zeppelin. So why must I be compelled to stand in ceremony and praise the gods of rock when they could care less about me anyway? So I stand by those grand sweeping proclamations, the self-assured and gloriously obnoxious-sounding statements. Simply because the fact that we've been able to release several albums and people still want to hear them is a testament to what we've achieved and to the respect and trust we fought tooth and nail to earn from our audience.

I've been tenacious and filled with ambition for as long as I can remember. But I was never concerned with making an acceptance speech at the Emmys or the Grammys. Those were never my goals. Sure, it'd be cool if those things happened. But all that truly matters to me is that I get to do more and more every year. The stage show must grow more massive. The time I'm able to spend making a record gets longer. Give me the resources to expend all of my energy in there, working like a mad scientist. That's it.

How can I see anything but a remarkable trajectory? I have no real education and no brothers or sisters. I have my parents, my wife, her family, and the art that I've created.

It would be soul-crushingly devastating to look at my life as anything other than a success, and in my darkest moments, that was my biggest obstacle. I'd lose sight of just how cool my life had indeed become. Anytime I sat at home moping about how things weren't going my way, it was because I'd lost the plot about what mattered.

I have great things in my life and even more incredible opportunities opening up all of the time. When I've looked at what someone else has and wanted it for myself, I've always viewed it as something to attain through hard work and dedication versus something to ruminate over with envy. If it means that much to me, I should work toward getting it.

To operate under the idea that I'm incapable of achieving this or that or lamenting that I don't have what someone else has is the ultimate in self-defeat. The attitude that I *can and will* make something happen is ninety-nine percent of the battle. I'm not a trained actor or a gifted singer. I never worked as a television presenter. These weren't things I could list on a résumé as part of my skillset. But I knew I could do them if I earned the chance.

When someone else has something, they were given it or they worked for it. When I was younger, full of anger, there was nothing I hated more than the spoiled kid from the wealthy family. Because they got to do everything they ever wanted simply because they won life's lottery. If it wasn't given to *me*, then it's time for me to get to work.

The more I resolve to work harder, the less resentful I've been about people who seem to have it easy. And we can't know someone else's struggle, anyway.

A few years ago if someone would tell me this or that young band on the ascent was handed opportunities

Black Veil Brides had to fight tooth and nail to even get close to, it would elicit a longwinded rant from me about the importance of hard work. Now I'll hear this sort of thing and think to myself, "Eh? Why should I care? I can't stop that wheel from turning, so why should I waste time thinking about it?"

I hope I get to do this for as long as I want to do it. I want to be the one who decides when it's time to retire. I don't want to have to quit because the bottom dropped out. I should be so lucky to become someone who can tour consistently and have an audience that's interested in what I'm doing when I'm past the age where most people choose to retire.

I'm not unaware of the fact that many of the artists that have been on the covers of the same magazines I have are no longer "relevant" or in some cases even together. Plenty of bands go from thousands to hundreds to dozens of people in the audience after years of coming through the same towns. Decades from now, I'd love to be still answering emails about what kind of stage production I want on the next tour. I never want to lose my grip on the connection between the person I was as a child and the person I will eventually grow to become. It was all I ever wanted. The song "Heart of Fire" is about that passion and my steadfast determination to keep that flame burning as brightly as ever.

How interesting is it to have a life predicated on something that for most people is antiquated? I'm in an excellent position. I don't ever want to be one of those

THEY DON'T NEED TO UNDERSTAND

musicians wandering around a festival, mean-mugging the younger bands because I'm bitter or jealous. I never want to live as if the simple act of being myself is burdensome to me.

As Paul Stanley once said: "That's like winning the lottery and then complaining about the taxes. Or becoming president and saying, 'I don't like wearing a tie.'"

It's also a mistake when bands say they don't care what people think about them. The important thing is to care about what the *right* people think—to listen to them, to maintain an audience without pandering. I care about the people around me, the people in my inner circle, and the people that allow me to do what I love for a living.

As for the rest of them, they don't need to understand.